Dedication

To my wife, Letitia

Contents

Foreword

It is a privilege to commend Alan Kolp's study of George Fox (1624-1691), founder of the Society of Friends. As an Anglican of the catholic/sacramental variety, I am struck how one age can illuminate another, how a different tradition helps me understand more fully my own, how an encounter with someone totally different from myself can light up the depths of my soul. I have always held the Quakers in the highest esteem, partly because of the experience of "radical mutuality" of my tradition with theirs. I hope I will not be misunderstood if I say that I see the Society of Friends as a sort of religious order within the great Church Catholic. Their witness is important for the whole church. I find that Quakers are biblically grounded without being fundamentalist or literalist, and, in spite of the absence of liturgy in the traditional sense, they display a gracious, inclusive and sacramental sensibility to the world. Quakers know, above all, how to be *present* and make that presence heal and make a difference. They love. They care. They challenge.

Christianity has often been called "The School of Love." This *sounds* wonderful, but in practice people prefer rules and regulations to the freedom of love. While love is, in a sense, "beyond rules" it still needs to be ordered and regulated if it is to be truly free. The first rule of the spiritual life is *accuracy*—telling the truth. George Fox was a spiritual master who understood the necessity of a properly ordered loving based on accuracy. Was he a perfectionist? I suppose he was—but not in the deadly way we have come to understand the word. To him perfection was a gift. It is all grace. Fox appreciated and celebrated the sheer giftedness of things. He searched for inner light and peace during a period of unusual and violent upheaval. Perhaps that is one of the reasons George Fox speaks so clearly to us today. In times of crisis people tend to exchange theological, political or therapeutic slogans rather than struggle to "speak the truth in love." Fox sets us a good example.

Our world is threatened by greed and tribalism, and needs a society of friends as surely as an England torn apart by a civil war which culminated in the beheading of a king in 1649. It was soon after the execution of Charles I that the beginning of Quakerism is traditionally celebrated. In 1652 Fox climbed Pendle Hill and received a vision of his ministry. That vision included a highly intuitive appreciation of the dynamism of the spiritual life as a movement from the Ocean of Darkness into the Ocean of Light. His was, if you will, an apocalyptic vision of our earthly pilgrimage—gentler but no less challenging than that of his contemporary John Bunyan (1628-1688). Bunyan's is a brilliant exposition of the inner life as spiritual warfare; Fox's is our initiation into a new creation with a glimpse of paradise. His vision is enough to make anyone *quake*! He took sin seriously but he identified it with idolatry, illusion and death rather than with the breaking of rules. His analysis of repentance was such that he not only saw the despair at the heart of the human drama but also the power of God to shake us out of darkness and into light.

Here we have a tough spirituality of transformation. I am reminded of the admonition in the Prologue to *The Cloud of Unknowing* where the author urges the reader not to share the book with people who are not ready for it: "I do not mind at all if the loud-mouthed, or flatterers, or the mock-modest, or fault-finders, gossips, tittle-tattlers, talebearers, or any sort of grumbler, never see this book!" So it is with George Fox. I wonder how many of us dare pay heed to his challenge? How many of us expect the unexpected in the way that he did?

What attracts me most to Fox are his unsentimental cheerfulness, and his self (or better) God-confidence which gave him the courage to be accessible to everyone he met. Alan Kolp rightly connects the wisdom of George Fox with that of contemporary writers, for example with Thomas Merton. I could not help being struck by certain echoes in Fox of St. Teresa of Avila, whose psychological and spiritual insight throws light on our spiritual progress through the Interior Castle. Both the Quaker and the Roman Catholic knew what it was like to live a lie and be a stranger in one's own house (soul).

I can think of no better way to conclude the preface to this work on George Fox than by quoting a fellow member of the Society of Friends, James Nayler (1616-1660): "There is a spirit which I feel that delights to do no evil, nor to revenge any wrong, but delights to endure all things, in hope to enjoy its own in the end." God's purpose for us is joy and delight and this book is a testimony to God's mission among us.

Alan Jones,
Grace Cathedral, San Francisco

x

Acknowledgements

Fresh Winds of the Spirit was initially encouraged and nurtured by two communities. Earlham School of Religion has been a wonderful place to teach. It has given me the opportunity primarily to attend to the area of spirituality. My work has been both to develop spirituality as an academic discipline in the seminary and to offer applied spirituality in local meetings and churches. The seminary made a space for writing this book by granting me a sabbatical leave in 1987-88. To both faculty and students I am deeply grateful.

The second community was the place of origin for the book. During my sabbatical year I was interim pastor of First Friends Meeting in Richmond, IN. The members of the meeting were responsive to explore in practical ways how Quaker spirituality can still express itself vibrantly when the Spirit's fresh winds blow. During the afternoons of that year countless alive and spirited persons came by the study with words of encouragement and support. To First Friends I am also grateful.

Besides these two groups of people there are others who need singly to be mentioned. Without the healing attention of Drs. Lawrence Einhorn, Stephen Williams, Anne Greist and Craig Nichols of Indiana University Hospital, no book would have been possible. Because the book is here, I can express appreciation for the easy working relationship with Ardith Talbot, Friends United Press Editor and Manager. A special word of thanks goes to Patricia Edwards, herself an academician and Quaker pastor, for skillfully editing the book to make it more readable. Finally, my deepest debt of gratitude goes to Sue Kern of Earlham School of Religion. Her cheerfulness stayed present through various drafts and her willingness to go the second mile of helpfulness touched me.

The gratitude having been expressed, I dedicate this book to my wife, Letitia. She has been an encouraging presence since undergraduate days at Guilford College. We have walked where George Fox walked; we climbed Pendle Hill in England with one daughter, Christina, in a backpack and the other daughter, Felicity, running ahead on her own. But, as the book will show, Quaker spirituality owes little to places and even less to things. People are key and so I dedicate this book to Letitia.

January 13, 1991
300th anniversary of George Fox's death
January 13, 1691, in London with these words
"I am clear, I am fully clear."

Preface

"I do not know why supposedly religious people are embarrassed at the thought of being born again."[1] No doubt, one of life's ironies is the realization that being born again is not only an experience of infancy. We scoff with Nicodemus at Jesus by asking, "How can a man be born when he is old?" (John 3:4) Jesus proceeds to say that we have to be born from above to enter the kingdom. Nicodemus finally is brought to the place of openness when he asks, "How can this be?" (John 3:9)

Presumably Nicodemus began to learn—to learn how he experientially could be born from above by the Spirit and come into the kingdom which Jesus proclaimed. Certainly, George Fox experienced this transforming spiritual presence about which he wrote. This book offers spiritual scrutiny to understand how being born into the kingdom takes place. In a Christian culture the kingdom is surprisingly strange and unfamiliar. In his introduction of his book, *The Silence of Jesus,* James Breech talks about finding the exceptional and original in Jesus. These words aptly apply to Fox— or any other spiritual person. "I would have to do everything possible to prepare myself for discovering the unexpected. This might seem a contradiction in terms, but in fact learning how to apprehend what is strange and unfamiliar is the most difficult discipline of all."[2]

The thought of discipline puts off many in our contemporary age. To put what Breech says in a different way is to say that learning about the Spirit's ways in the lives of people is, as Graham Greene has it, "learning to see things with a saint's eye."[3] In his novel, *The Power and the Glory,* Greene has a scene in an overcrowded, squalid jail. There the whiskey priest who is being pursued by the government finds himself talking to a rather piously prim woman. All the while in the dark regions across the room come the sounds of a stranger couple making love. Disgust is the feeling the pious one has for the apparently absurd couple. But the priest says to her:

'Such a lot of beauty. Saints talk about the beauty of suffering. Well, we are not saints, you and I. Suffering to us is just ugly. Stench and overcrowding and pain. *That* is beautiful in the corner—to them. It needs a lot of learning to see things with a saint's eye: a saint gets a subtle taste for beauty and can look down on poor ignorant palates like theirs. But we can't afford to.'[4]

Spirituality has to do with the totality of this scene—the sacred and the seemingly profane.

There is much in the spirituality of George Fox which is strange and unfamiliar. Even for Quakers who stand in a tradition grounded in the experience and theology of Fox, he still seems eccentric. This challenge, as his life speaks forth in his journal, continues to compel and upset. The radical faith proclaimed with public zeal and lived with energy always does.

Simply put, this book interprets the spirituality of George Fox by means of contemporary perspectives on the spiritual journey. Drawing heavily, but not exclusively on Roman Catholicism's balanced sense of the categories of spiritual development, one can understand Fox's spiritual experience in fresh ways. In turn, there is a genius to Fox's spiritual life which is repeatedly acknowledged in non-Quaker books on spirituality. This book will allow the non-Quaker to grasp Fox's genius in an organized, cohesive fashion.

Those in the widest audience who love Thomas Merton or are instructed by Henri Nouwen will find a soul-mate in George Fox. His spirituality will touch you with the warmth that only grace conveys. It will ground you with the confidence that only truth provides. It will embolden you with the courage that only hope generates. Finally, it will fire you with passion that only God's love excites.

Introduction
What Is Spirituality?

> The very term "spirituality" is a little awesome to Quakers ...
> Quakers find it hard not to look with suspicion on talk about
> the interior life and about the practices that nurture it.
>   However understandable this shyness may be with its at-
> tempt to avoid the pharisaical display of their alleged virtue,
> which in our generation they know to be greatly exagger-
> ated, the plain fact is that they do possess a spirituality of their
> own.[1]

Nearly one hundred years ago (1899-1900) at the University of
Berlin, the famous German theologian and church historian,
Adolf von Harnack delivered a series of public lectures on "The
Essence of Christianity." When translated into English, they were
entitled, *What Is Christianity?*[2] Nearly a century later, the question
is not "what is Christianity?" but "what is spirituality?"

This book focuses on spirituality. Spirituality is "in the air!" Indeed,
that is appropriate for the Greek word, *pneuma,* and the Latin word,
spiritus, both which can be translated as spirit and as air or wind. So,
spiritus and *spiritualis* (spiritual) are as present as wind, as common-
place as the air. At this level of spirit, wind, air, one begins. Unless
one knows a little about the wind and the spirit, then one will likely
miss the blowing of the fresh winds of spirit.

The late Episcopal theologian, Urban T. Holmes, opens his book,
Spirituality for Ministry, with a catchy story which illustrates both the
popularity of the word, spirituality, as well as how easily it can be
parodied.

> It has been my experience that one does not drop the word
> "spiritual" into a conversation lightly. "How is your spiritual
> life?" I unwittingly asked a minister in the presence of some
> others. There was a sudden, discernable tension in the air,
> as if I had inquired into the intimate details of his sex life.

Someone coughed and the person of whom I inquired, obviously sharing the embarrassment, felt he had to say something to me. After all, I was a fellow pastor. "Great," he said with an enthusiasm tinged with condescension. "I've really gotten it all together." Somehow getting it together" — the tired jargon of humanistic psychology was not what I had in mind, but now aware that I was treading on forbidden territory, I let it pass.[3]

This book is not going to let it pass. Instead, it will speed headlong into what spirituality is all about. "Getting it together" is an illusory invitation. Getting it together would mean worrying about living the spiritual life so it does not get messed up!

This book is about getting one's spiritual hair messed up—messed up because one has stepped outside into the wind of God's Spirit. Spirituality is the feel on one's face in a spring wind. It stirs in one the vigor of new birth. It brings youthful energy and spontaneity. It is the feeling of freshness which comes from that brisk encounter with God's north wind. Spirituality is perceptive to the gentle summer breezes which move ever-so-gently across the green leaves making the trees seem easily at movement. This gentle west wind nurtures the growth and development of the human spirit. Spirituality is the beautifully tender maturing into God's call. It brings the human spirit into the fruitfulness which autumn winds cultivate. The warm south winds bring appropriate mildness to this time of productivity. Finally, spirituality is the giving over to God all that one is and all that one has. It is a giving over continually in ministry and, ultimately, in death itself. It is the celebration of the cold east wind on one's face as it becomes clear that death is swallowed up in God's light and love. Spirituality, then, is not about getting it together but getting out into God's wind, to feel again those fresh winds of the Spirit.

Unfortunately, so many people in the western world live life trying to "get it together." Usually, this has little to do with feeling God's fresh winds of the Spirit. For example, on American television recently the theme of the advertisement for a deodorant called "Dry Idea" was, "never let them see you sweat." This illustrates the absurdity of having it all together. In this sense, having it all together meant not being normal, since sweating is normal, and at a deeper level, being non-human.

Wittingly or unwittingly, religion has often participated in the making of non-humans. From the twentieth century perspective one can laugh at paganism and child sacrifice. And yet, all too often religion has asked blacks and others of color to sacrifice their "self." In this case, slave owners made them work so hard everyone could see them sweat. Also, women have too frequently been asked to sacrifice self. But, to identify the "self" is to have come to the core concern of spirituality.

Spirituality concerns my-"self" in its authentic, true constitution; it is about the making of humans. Spirituality also asks for sacrifice—the sacrifice of the old self, the self fabricated by manipulative commercials—and demands the sacrifice of the self coercively created by a culture which denies or is otherwise out of touch with God. Spirituality is the human search for and discovery of God, or, it is the human realization God has sought and found us. In her novel, *The Color Purple*, Alice Walker has Shug doing theology. Shug says:

> God is inside you and inside everybody else. You come into the world with God. But only them that search for it inside find it. And sometimes it just manifests itself even if you not looking, or don't know what you looking for.[4]

Fresh winds of the Spirit are blowing. They are blowing inside you and everybody else. This book will help you find it. It will help those who are searching for God, and it will suggest how God is manifested even when folks are not looking for it.

One pits Walker's account of the divine search for humanity and humanity's seeking God against the well-known line from Thoreau's *Walden* when he declared that "the mass of men lead lives of quiet desperation. What is called resignation is confirmed desperation."[5] Spirituality is the antidote to this confirmed desperation. It is the word of hope spoken in a world of plenty, but where there is no meaning in the 'more'. Spirituality is the opportunity for faith when routine spells despair in the mass of people. Spirituality is an invitation to love when there are nothing but cold embers of apathy. "So to say that human beings are spiritual creatures is to suggest that they are capable of possessing the presence of the life-giving God."[6]

If humans are essentially spiritual creatures and if humans are capable of possessing the presence of the life-giving God, what has gone wrong? In a flip way, one can suggest culture has substituted a "dry idea" for the "true idea!" In humanity's quest to let no one see them sweat, sadly no one *sees* them. The true self has become hidden, invisible and lost. The truly human has disappeared. Boys and girls are made in the image of parents, then teachers, then peer groups and work forces. Men and women are remade in the image of Madison Avenue. Malcolm Muggeridge captures something of this in his 1976 London Lectures in Contemporary Christianity. With an acid look at our way of living Muggeridge proclaims ours to be:

> A cult of consumption; the supermarkets with soft music playing, its temples; the so-persuasive voices, "'Buy this! Eat this! Wear this! Drink this!" of priests and priestesses; the transformation wrought by adopting such a diet, using such gadgets, stretching out on such a bed, the miracles; with Muzak for plainsong, computers for oracles, cash-registers ringing in the offertory - so, they will conclude, the worship of the great god Consumption was conducted, with seemly reverence and dedication. There were even religious orders, with prodigies in the way of asceticism being performed in the interest of slimming and otherwise beautifying the male and female person.[7]

Muggeridge offers a perceptive clue about one's "self," the my-"self" which is rediscovered after sacrificing the Madison-"self."

Appropriately, spirituality and Madison Avenue advertising both talk in images. Images are the cue to the self. Madison Avenue creates and manipulates a false self; spirituality reminds one that humans are created in God's image and are capable of possessing the presence of the life-giving God in whose image they are created. However, because of the success of the fabrication of the false self, people have come to assume what is normal and routine is true! Muggeridge slices through this temptation when he notes:

> The prevailing impression I have come to have of the contemporary scene is of an ever-widening chasm between the fantasy in terms of which the media induce us to live, and the reality of our existence as made in the image of God, as sojourners in time whose true habitat is eternity. The fantasy is all encompassing; awareness of reality requires the seeing eye which comes to those born again in Christ. It is like coming to after an anaesthetic, the mists lift, consciousness

returns, everything in the world is more beautiful than ever it was, because related to a reality beyond the world - every thought clearer, love deeper, joy more abounding, hope more certain.[8]

Spirituality, then, is the rediscovery that humans are made in God's image. Spirituality is the acquisition of this "seeing eye" which comes as the result of God's gift of rebirth. For Quakers and all Christians, Jesus Christ experientially plays a central role in this spiritual re-birthing process.

Parker Palmer declares "there is no such thing as 'spirituality in general.' Every spiritual search is and must be guided by a particular literature, practice, and community of faith."[9] This book's particular focus is specifically the Christian spirituality shaped by George Fox (1624-1691). Appropriately, Fox is celebrated as the founding father of the Quaker movement and Fox's *Journal* as the primary text.[10] But more importantly, he developed a spirituality which still speaks to the condition of humans on the eve of the twenty-first century. The spirituality which emerged out of Fox's life and ministry is significant precisely because it still speaks and still offers a challenging option to the fantasy of media lives.

Because of Fox's contemporary relevance, this book is not con-cerned with the history of George Fox nor of Quakerism. Nor is the concern primarily with his theology. Both of these have received adequate attention over the years. What has not been addressed, is Fox's spirituality. His spirituality, like any spirituality, is an expression of how God is experienced. One looks closely at the language, the images, the metaphors to hear, to see, to feel, to taste, to touch the fabric of the experience with the divine. Hence, one comes to the heart of what spirituality is: experience.

In her recent book, *Spirituality and Personal Maturity,* Joann Wolski Conn says "spirituality refers to both lived experience and an academic discipline."[11] In this book, the focus is on the lived expe-rience. The adjective "lived" is an important addition to the heart of the spiritual experience. Quakers have long held that theology begins with experience; here one appropriately notes spirituality is rooted in lived experience. Theology is reflection on one's experience; spirituality is the lived experience. It is the cultivation and nurturing of ongoing, lived experience in, from and with God's Spirit. Spiritu-ality is the story in lived experiences of how God forms humans in the divine image. Indeed, to "get into" spirituality is to get into someone's story. This book does precisely that: it gets into Fox's story.

Looking into Fox's story, one can see first-hand how God formed his spirit, reformed him into Christ's image and transformed his person into a new self. This new self went about England and beyond proclaiming and exclaiming what God had done and would do. This self-expression came out of his spirituality; indeed, this self-expression was his spirituality, his lived experience. Fox's spiritual self-expression contrast with so much in the contemporary world. Abraham Heschel, a Jewish theologian, notes the twentieth century's need for this kind of self-expression.

> There was never a time in which the need for self-expression was so much stressed. Yet, there was never a time in which self-expression was so rarely achieved; in which there was so much pressure to adjust oneself to conventions, cliches, to vogue and standardization. The self is silent; words are dead, and prayer is a forgotten language.[12]

In his own contemporary way, Heschel points to the current human dilemma in much of western society. Western women and men paradoxically are doing so well and failing so miserably! Further words from Heschel (preserving the non-inclusive language when quoting) observes that:

> Man has become a forgotten thing. We know his desires, his whims, his failings; we do not know his ultimate commitment. We understand what he *does*, we do not understand what he *means*. We stand in awe of many things; we do not know what we stand for.[13]

Humans made by media and manipulated by monsters have no true self to express and, sadly, become forgotten things. This raises the question of this book: so, what can any person do?

Spirituality is as much the question as it is an answer. If spirituality is lived experience, then there are questions which need to be asked. Indeed, Christian spirituality has to do with being in the place to ask questions of ultimate commitment and meaning. Wendy Wright tells the story of her encounter with a Trappist novice master and how that centralized the role of the question.

I am reminded of a Trappist novice master I once met who commented that to be a Christian is not to know the answers but to be a person who is able to live in the part of the self where the question exists. There, in the birthplace of all the questions - not simply the critical analytical questions but the painful urgings of human aspiration that press us forward, crying out for guidance, mercy, and justice - there we are born along with our questioning. It is a creative place that forms us anew, making us in the image of our god ... [14]

Spirituality is the work of the divine Spirit forming one anew in the creative place known as the human heart. There is where the image of God is found and where it is re-shaped. Spirituality begins with our birth into this divine Spirit—this is always one's answer, to be born again and again. But one is not merely born into the Spirit. One is also born along with the Spirit. In this bearing along come the questions because life is open ended. So, spirituality is the lived experience of being born into the Spirit and born along with the Spirit.

If spirituality brings humans into the sphere of God's Spirit and lets them experience the flow of that Spirit moving through their lives, then it is easy to see why Murray Bodo, Franciscan spiritual director, defines spirituality as simply the "*art of growing closer to God.*"[15] This is an intriguing way to understand that spirituality means seeing a personal, spiritual story such as Fox's is like watching an artist paint a picture. Spirituality is an art; one practices the art by the way lived experiences are shaped, molded, fashioned and created. The Latin word for art, *artis*, very well conveys what is at stake. An art is the ability to make or do something. Spirituality, as an art, is the ability to be in relationship with the divine Spirit who creates one and, then, calls one into relationship which gives life meaning and destiny a sense of purpose.

Spirituality, as an art, is more than just having the ability to be in relationship with God; it is the art of growing closer to God and involves the shaping of ability with knowledge and the development of skills. This is where George Fox is an exquisite artist. Because of his quest to grow closer to God and God's gracing of his quest, one can truly behold a work of art: his life!

Indeed, this work of art is captured in the fullest sense of the Latin word, *artis*, meaning a way of life. Looking at Fox's way of life, one sees spirituality as an art of growing closer to God. From that clues emerge to guide contemporary women and men in their spiritual pilgrimages. George Fox's life story enables contemporary pilgrims walking through life to know where God is.

Instructively, where God is for us is not different than it was for Fox. His experience is valuable because he knew where God is and then, shared his lived experience. In the words of Bodo:

> ... God is "in," not simply "out there." He is in things, in people, in relationships, in our efforts to build a better society, in struggle and pain, in me, in my body, in my emotions and longings, in my maleness or femaleness, and in the world. And the great asceticism is in finding God where he is.[16]

Fox and Quakers have always known God is "in" as well as "out there." To practice the art of growing closer to God is not only to know where God is but to live in and from that place. To practice that art is to be whole and holy.

Too frequently, one only knows something by being acquainted with its opposite. In today's world Mother Teresa is mentioned to describe what holiness is. And yet, few people have any direct acquaintance with Mother Teresa and little knowledge about holiness. One can do better by beginning to recall people who exhibit characteristics of profanity, people who disdain the divinity and betray the grace of holiness. This is the kind of person whom Heschel describes as the one:

> ...who betrays Him (God) day after day, drunk with vanity, resentment, or reckless ambition, lives in a ghostly mist of misgivings. Having ruined love with greed, he is still wondering about the lack of tenderness in his own life. His soul contains a hiding-place for an escaping conscience. He has torn his ties to God into shreds of shrieking dread, and his mind remains dull and callous. Spoiler of his own lot, he walks the earth a skeleton of a soul, raving about missed delight.[17]

This kind of profanity is the contemporary version of Thoreau's mass of people living lives of quiet desperation. Their lived experience is one of fragmentation, unhappiness and bondage. They are not artists of the Spirit, but technicians of torment and dealers in deadness.

Spirituality is the process of transforming this deadness into new life. Theological words that describe this process rightly can be called salvation. But spirituality is more than a theological slogan; in fact, the jargon is itself often the problem instead of the solution. More than theology, spirituality is the lived experience of putting meat on the bones of the soul's skeleton.

Spirituality is the transforming work of bringing wholeness and integrity into the fragmentation of the profane person who has spoiled his or her lot. It is the graceful work of God who enters into every person's Egypt and leads out of the bondage which characterizes life there. Spirituality is the proclamation that there is a God and the reclamation that one can know this God. As Thomas Kelly wrote in his Quaker classic, *A Testament of Devotion,* "within the silences of the souls of men an eternal drama is ever being enacted ... and always its chief actor is - the Eternal God of Love." [18]

Quaker spirituality is one particular way of life, one particular spiritual art form to understand the human interaction with this God of love. This book finally is less interested in presenting George Fox and more in using him to show what God has done and will do. Quakers have a "real" name which is preferable to the nickname, "Quakers." They are the Religious Society of Friends. Traditionally, this naming of Friends is rooted in the biblical text where Jesus addressed his disciples saying, "No longer do I call you servants, for the servant does not know what his master is doing; but I have called you friends..." (John 15:15) The lovely part of this text is the fact that the Greek word here translated as "friends" is *philos,* one of three Greek words for love. So, literally, by this new relationship with Jesus who is the Word incarnate, these disciples have encountered and entered the sphere of divine love. For God so loved the world that in Jesus, God set about making friends.

As the Religious Society of Friends, Quakers live out an experience of this love making. Quaker spirituality is at heart a deep expression of Christian spirituality, an ongoing story of God's passionate love for all the world. This is the drama, as Kelly calls it, by which God as lover continually and persuasively is calling each to become sons and daughters, and friends with God and each other.

Quaker spirituality, lived and articulated by Fox, is an embodiment of the Christian gospel. For Fox and early Friends this gospel was a lived experience with the God of love, which challenged everything else which masqueraded as religion and, one might add, still does today. Walter Wink captures this brilliantly: "fidelity to the gospel lies not in repeating its slogans but in plunging the prevailing idolatries into its corrosive acids."[19] Fox gives a sustained look at how a person experienced the good news of God's love, made friends with this Jesus and set about in ministry to other friends. From England to foreign shore, societies of Friends were gathered. Wherever Fox and others went, they traveled in fidelity to this everlasting gospel of love-making.

This gospel is acidic to the idolatries of the world. The gospel in which spirituality takes root is always paradoxical. This gospel condemns the idolatries of any prevailing culture while proclaiming the love of God. God continues to seek out those who are conditioned by idolatries not to know God! As Parker Palmer states, "the world creates the self by means of conditioning..."[20] God re-conditions!

Spirituality, then, is the lived experience by which God incarnationally and gracefully intervenes in this worldly conditioning. This lived experience of coming to know God re-conditions everybody's situation so that a new "self" is born, and the old self dies. Re-conditioned from one's personal and social world, one steps free from this never-ending running after other gods. Persons become free—free to love God, free to love self, free to love others.

George Fox was born into this freedom and given to this kind of love. This book tells his story, not the historical or theological story, but the spiritual story. In that sense, it is not just his story; it is everyone's story. His story was lived with such vigor and told with such clarity that it energizes and informs everyone else's story. So, in this book share Fox's story as it reveals your story.

I

THE OCEAN OF DARKNESS

And the Lord answered that it was needful I should have a
sense of all conditions, how else should I speak to all
conditions; and in this I saw the infinite love of God. I saw
also that there was an ocean of darkness and death, but an
infinite ocean of light and love, which flowed over the ocean
of darkness.[1]

The ocean of darkness is simply one phrase among many which
Fox used to describe the reality of the human spirit in its alienation
from God. As a young man, Fox experienced this alienation in deep
and profound ways. Reading him, one can glimpse the paths of a man
who was stretched to the limit. The miracle of his story is that he did
not commit suicide but rather was found by God. He narrates
something about both the nature of the human spirit and the nature
of the God who finally saves us from ourselves. At the heart of this
"saving" is an encounter, a genuine spiritual experience which
becomes the lived experience of spirituality.

The ocean of darkness is a compelling metaphor used by Fox to
express both the recognition of alienation from God and also the
feeling of this distance. In a highly intellectual fashion, Sallie
McFague describes the features of a metaphor: "a metaphor is an
assertion or judgment of similarity and difference between two

thoughts in permanent tension with one another, which redescribes reality in an open-ended way but has structural as well as effective power."[2] In less academic terms, McFague is saying to us that a metaphor, in this case the "ocean of darkness," is making an assertion about one thing (humanity's alienation from God, in language drawn from another, ordinary realm (large bodies of water and the absence of light.) Indeed, there is nothing inherently theological or spiritual about either ocean or darkness. But, by beginning to "see" the way these two words point to something beyond water and absence of light, then one is in the place where one might be moved (affected). Further, there are some ways structurally by which this metaphorical language, "ocean of darkness," can begin to color and direct not only one's experience but even thinking about that experience. At this point, one has entered into the realm of Fox's spirituality by means of his language.

Gerald May, noted psychiatrist and spiritual director, has said that the:

> ...real importance of spiritual experiences can be considered only in terms of how they change and affect our lives in relation to God, ourselves, and each other. In part, these changes depend upon how we integrate and respond to the experiences. In spiritual direction it is necessary to examine such effects and responses carefully, rather than focusing simply on the content of an experience.[3]

This is exactly what one can do with Fox. Not only does he share a great deal about his spiritual experience, but he also gives an analyst the chance to examine carefully the effects and responses of his spiritual experience. In this sense, Fox is not simply the founder of the Religious Society of Friends, or Quakers, but becomes, more importantly, a spiritual director for our time.

Alan Jones captures well the flamboyant character of the true spiritual director.

> The director has been called 'the disciplined wild man.' We should note that he is disciplined, not tamed. He is a pilgrim himself, a wounded healer...He does not set himself up as an expert. He sees himself as a companion to others, subject to the same hurts and temptations. Loneliness, self-contempt, moral ambiguity attack him as much as any one else.[4]

There is little doubt the crucial, formative time for Fox in this ocean of darkness were the years 1643-1647. This is the period Fox began his formation which enables him to be a spiritual director for our time. Suffering severe depression, his writing betrays a depth of anguish which still pulls at the soul of the reader. Fox was nineteen when he entered this tumultuous period. Before 1643, he had been a good but serious boy. His journal narrates that "in my very young years I had a gravity and stayedness of mind and spirit not usual in children."[5] As he approached adolescence, he continued in this serious vein. "When I came to eleven years of age, I knew pureness and righteousness; for while I was a child I was taught how to walk to be kept pure."[6] As Fox neared the end of his teen-age years, this solemnity took a deeper turn.

Contemporary terminology might quickly recognize that Fox was merely trying to find out who he was. His was an identity quest. But his quest for identity was, more importantly, a quest for a spiritual identity. As it turned out, he discovered who he was only by discovering who God was. In this, he is not far from the kind of experience Thomas Merton in our own century describes.

> The only true joy on earth is to escape from the prison of our own false self, and enter by love into union with the Life Who dwells and sings within the essence of every creature and in the core of our own souls. In His love we possess all things and enjoy fruition of them, finding Him in them all. And thus, as we go about the world, everything we meet and everything we see and hear and touch, far from defiling, purifies us and plants in us something more of contemplation and of heaven.[7]

Using Merton's language, Fox was able to escape from the prison of his false self. Fox knew this false self not as a "god" self, but as an alienated, dark, depressed self. During those years, Fox struggled with this false self and through the love of God was united with the creator and redeemer. In a word, God planted Fox in heaven! Tracing this journey is to know experientially something of that heaven.

The seriousness of this period was signaled in the beginning. Fox tells us that "at the command of God, on the 9th day of the Seventh Month (September), 1643, I left my relations and broke off all familiarity or fellowship with young or old."[8] The decisiveness of this moment, the attribution of its motivation to the command of God and the duration of the search all arrest anyone in the twentieth century who want rewarding experiences quickly and painlessly! Fox began this quest and paid a price, but gladly, for he had found himself and found God. The lived experience of spirituality is not always painless or quick, but it is rewarding because it is so deeply meaningful. The power of the exacted price once more speaks.

> Now during all this time I was never joined in profession of religion with any, but gave up myself to the Lord, having forsaken all evil company, and taken leave of father and mother and all other relations, and travelled up and down as a stranger in the earth...[9]

The experience of heeding God's command to forsake all estranged Fox from all. It left him literally on a journey travelling around England and figuratively, on a spiritual journey as a stranger on the earth.

Indeed, Fox does seem strange! In his search for God he broke off with familiarity and conformity. He placed himself beyond civilization as he knew it and chose alien status, a foreigner. As an alien he set out looking for a spiritual home. He was a stranger seeking a friend. In this process he quit looking externally and peered inside his own self. The question was posed: would he remain strange and alien to himself?

In this experience of being a stranger Fox realized how alone he was. The themes of stranger, alien and being alone coalesce around a *feeling of despair.* It is in the mire of near-despair that Fox came to terms with who he was and he discovered who God was and how God was for him. The depth of his despair is captured in these poignant words:

> Now during the time that I was at Barnet a strong temptation to despair came upon me. And then I saw how I was tempted, and mighty troubles I was in. And sometimes I kept myself retired in my chamber, and often walked solitary in the Chase there, to wait upon the Lord. And I wondered why these things should come to me; and I looked upon myself and said, 'Was I ever so before?' Then I thought, because I

had forsaken my relations I had done amiss against them; so
I was brought to call to mind all my time that I had spent and
to consider whether I had wronged any. But temptations
grew more and more and I was tempted almost to despair...[10]

Notice that Fox never actually surrendered to the despair itself; he
never gave up.
Literally, to despair is to be without hope, to give up. What Fox
experienced in this dark night was the temptation to say there is no
hope, the temptation to give up. He did not experience despair, but
the *temptation* to despair. In this he appropriately saw himself as an
imitator of Christ. In this formative experience Fox was being called
to submit to a process of loosing his false self and being born into a
new self. In the midst of this transformation, what was tested was
more than his trust in God but, whether *there was a God?* In the
process of transformation there is a scary point of decision where one
is not sure whether to give up the false self, the self formed after one's
own image or someone else's image. There, at that point, one is
tempted either to give up by holding on to the false self (illusion) or
to give up period (despair). Fox could not go back; hence, his
temptation was to despair.

Fox relates that he kept to himself in his room or walked solitary
in the surrounding area. This is not anti-social behavior, but spiritual
seeking. Fox was not looking for friends but for answers, and,
particularly, for an experience which would "answer his condition."
In fact, Fox was experiencing a dark night of the soul rather than
psychological depression. These are subtly different, but different
nevertheless.

Benedict Groecshel, contemporary writer on spirituality, describes
spiritual darkness as "a psychological state of great discomfort, pre-
cipitated either by external causes like a painful loss or trauma or by
inner conflicts leading to depression and a feeling of profound alienation."[11] Because there is a close relationship between the psychological and the spiritual, it seems clear that Fox was experiencing spiritual
darkness. His primary language is drawn from spirituality; however,
his experience as a person was also psychologically affected. Gerald
May delineates this distinction between the dark night of our soul and
our psychological experience of it. He says that our experiences of
the dark night "have no psychological causation, (but) there is bound
to be a psychological response. This response, which may include

fear, grief, despair, and not a little depression, needs to be seen as our reaction to noticing the dark night and not as a part of the dark night itself."[12]

Fox used the language of "condition" to describe his state of darkness and alienation from God, and was looking for someone with experience or wisdom who could speak to his condition. That he received misguided advice and uninformed direction is true; it would be comical if it were not so serious. In one account Fox lamments that:

> ...I went to another ancient priest at Mancetter in Warwick-shire and reasoned with him about the ground of despair and temptations, but he was ignorant of my condition; and he bid me take tobacco and sing psalms. Tobacco was a thing I did not love and psalms I was not in an estate to sing; I could not sing.[13]

Indeed, to be in a state or condition of darkness and alienation means one cannot sing. Singing goes with joy. If anything, Fox was only able to lament.

Lament is a form of poetry expressing sadness and loneliness. In the Hebrew Bible the book of Lamentations begins by reflecting on the sufferings of Jerusalem. "How lonely sits the city that was full of people!" (Lam. 1:1) Further, one reads that "she weeps bitterly in the night, tears on her cheeks." (Lam. 1:2) In his dark night of the soul, Fox lamented his condition. He wrote that, in spite of meeting with some friendly and tender people:

> ...my troubles continued, and I was often under great temp-tations; and I fasted much, and walked abroad in solitary places many days, and often took my Bible and went and sat in hollow trees and lonesome places till night came on; and frequently in the night walked mournfully about by myself, for I was a man of sorrows in the times of the first workings of the Lord in me.[14]

Suggestively, Fox interpreted his soul-searching as God's first work-ings. This is one more reason to understand his experience as a dark night, because in this spiritual process one can still be open to God's work in history; there is a sense of purpose and an openness to providence. In despair, purpose is lost and providence does not exist. Interestingly, Fox fasted as a way to be open to God's purpose and prepare for this providential working of the Lord.

To fast in this kind of space is like keeping your eyes open even when it is dark. In the ocean of darkness Fox kept his eyes open, continuing to look for that flicker of light and dim glimpse which would provide the opportunity to see. Unlike then, fasting as a spiritual discipline is little practiced today. Richard Foster proclaims, "in a culture where the landscape is dotted with shrines to the Golden Arches and an assortment of Pizza Temples, fasting seems out of place, out of step with the times."[15] Too quickly one might read over this reference to fasting and miss the "aim" of Fox's disciplined seeking. One gains an idea of what fasting may do when Foster continues:

> More than any other single Discipline, fasting reveals the things that control us. This is a wonderful benefit to the true disciple who longs to be transformed into the image of Jesus Christ. We cover up what is inside us with food and other good things, but in fasting these things surface.[16]

Through the self-denial of fasting, Fox opened himself to that image of God which would be experienced as an "answer," be seen as light and experienced as joy.

In addition to fasting, Fox also said he spent time alone. He walked in solitary places, sat in hollow trees and lonesome places until night came. He walked around in sadness by himself. This is not the picture of a man mired in melancholy, but the portrait of one who is wrestling with himself and who he is to become. Only in retrospect could he begin to see this was the first workings of the Lord. In the moment, Fox was daring to confront only himself and its truth—that maybe he was nothing, a nobody.

In the contemporary language of spirituality, he was *paying attention.* Alan Jones describes this in the context of simplifying one's way of living. Jones admonishes the disciple-to-be that:

> ...it is necessary to cultivate a simpler (not necessarily easier) way of living with ourselves based on an honest attentiveness to what is there, and on a sound knowledge of what makes us tick. The process of self-simplification can make

us very uncomfortable. The practice of simple attention will eventually bring us to the verge of tears.[17]

Fox was seriously and ardently practicing *simple attention*. He was looking, but not yet seeing. This tempted him to despair. He was mournful, but not ready to quit. The strength of Fox was not to quit, not to give up. Indeed, one does well to remember that this tempting period lasted four years! It is, finally, to a person alone that God will or will not speak, will be revealed or stay hidden. It was to this potential abyss that Fox exposed his self, waited to see if there were a God and if there would be a self which could sustain that knowing—either way! This tapped into his fear of loneliness, what Sebastian Moore calls the "inner loneliness." Moore says, "loneliness is how I feel when the world is silent to my question, 'Who am I?'"[18] In order to be transformed into the self God would one become, one has to risk—alone—the question "Who am I?" Most people remain content with their current false self, the self created after one's own image. Henri Nouwen describes this avenue of risk for those ready to ask the question.

In solitude I get rid of my scaffolding: no friends to talk with, no telephone calls to make, no meetings to attend, no music to entertain, no books to distract, just me—naked, vulnerable, weak, sinful, deprived, broken—nothing. It is this nothingness that I have to face in my solitude, a nothingness so dreadful that every thing in me wants to run to my friends, my work, and my distractions so I can forget my nothingness and make myself believe that I am worth something...The struggle is real because the danger is real. It is the danger of living the whole of our life as one long defense against the reality of our condition...That is the struggle. It is the struggle to die to the false self.[19]

In these contemporary words one glimpses the process of Fox's spiritual birth and transformation.

Solitude is that place where one risks self, risks one's very life as one knows it. Solitude is a place where one's past—one's false self will be burned as a bridge over which one tentatively walked. Nouwen declares that "solitude is the furnace of transformation. Without solitude we remain victims of our society and continue to be entangled in the illusions of the false self."[20] Nouwen's metaphor of furnace as the place where God meets one is expressed metaphorically by Fox as the ocean of darkness.

In the middle of a passage otherwise given over to proclaiming God's gracious transforming, Fox graphically recalls being stuck in this ocean of darkness.

> When I myself was in the deep, under all shut up, I could not believe that I should ever overcome; my troubles, my sorrows, and my temptations were so great, that I thought many times I should have despaired, I was so tempted.[21]

It is with the metaphor of the ocean of darkness and death and how Fox experienced it that one enters the mythology (story) of Quaker spirituality. This ocean and the "other" ocean of light and love are powerfully suggestive symbols and, hence, lure one into the nature of that reality. Fox is so meaningful because of the rich symbolic world he knows and offers. He created a movement and formed a people because of this spiritual journey and not because he went up Pendle Hill. Walter Wink summarizes well why the rich symbolism of Fox created a story which moved people out of their own deadness.

> Through a set of powerfully evocative symbols acknowledged as meaningful by people, (myth) presents an incredibly condensed story that depicts, through the indirect language of narrative, the nature of ultimate reality, the way things got how they are, the path to salvation, and the final meanings of life.[22]

With Fox's symbol of the ocean of darkness, one begins the exploration of his spirituality.

The image of being "in the deep" is the first clear feeling of the governing metaphor, "ocean of darkness." The literal ocean has many "deep" places. Indeed, for anyone who has traversed an ocean, the awareness of those deep places is not far away. In a boat or ship one plies the waters, safely floating above the deep. But, one knows simultaneously that one is "in" the water which itself constitutes "the deep!" And so, in a peculiar way, to be safely atop these waters is at the same time to be vulnerable to the very danger of these waters.

When Fox declared he was "in the deep," he meant he was trapped in the peril of his existence. Not claiming to be physically in danger for his life, he alarmingly confessed that a meaningful life was at stake. To be in the deep is to be in a place where one cannot see because the light cannot penetrate to one's condition. To be in the deep is to be "in" *so far* that even though one could move, one might never move far enough to be able to come "out."

The Psalmist uses the image of the deep, in a favorable way, a way which, at this juncture, Fox had not experienced. Psalm 42 is a lament psalm which begins appropriately for Fox in these despairing years. The Psalmist acknowledges, "as a heart longs for flowing streams, so longs my soul for Thee, O God. My soul thirsts for God, for the living God. When shall I come and behold the face of God?" (Ps. 42:1-2) Later, the Psalmist employs the image of "the deep." The Psalmist laments that his soul is cast down and, then says, "deep calls to deep at the thunder of thy cataracts; all Thy waves and Thy billows have gone over me. By day the Lord commands his steadfast love; and at night his song is with me, at prayer to the God of my life." (Ps. 42:7-8)

Fox was not yet experiencing "the deep calling to deep," and yet, oddly enough, he was at the right place—namely, the deep—to hear the call! So far, he was experiencing the deep as being "under all shut up." To be in the deep is to be under all. To be under all means that one is so far under one is "shut up." It is this sense of being shut up that introduces the element of despair, of hopelessness. To be in the ocean of darkness brings one to despair if one feels "under it all" and "shut up." To despair is to feel *impotent*—powerless to do anything that will make a difference!

As a root metaphor the ocean of darkness offers Fox many ways to describe his condition of alienation from God. Literally, the ocean leaves one wet if one steps into it. Figuratively, there are options. One option Fox employed to describe his condition was that it rendered him dry and barren. In an early account of seeking help from others, Fox told of his visit to "one Macham, a priest in high account." Fox continued:

> And he would needs give me some physic and I was to have been let blood, but they could not get one drop of blood from me, either in arms or head, though they endeavored it, my body being, as it were, dried up with sorrows, grief, and troubles...[23]

Quakers have historically talked about being in "dry" places or going through "dry periods." This language suggests being in a place or at a time when God's Spirit is experienced as absent. In his own way, Fox claimed that his search for help from the priest, Macham, was a plea to one who might show him the way to find God. Fox is not saying here that he was dead, but just as good as dead! To remain dry and barren finally would be to die.

Thomas Merton describes an entry point to contemplation that begins with a feeling of dryness and barrenness. Although the stage Merton describes usually occurs later in a spiritual pilgrimage, nevertheless, it helps to recognize the characteristics of dryness...

> The most usual entrance to contemplation is through a desert of aridity in which, although you see nothing and feel nothing and apprehend nothing and are conscious only of a certain interior suffering and anxiety, yet you are drawn and held in this darkness and dryness because it is the only place in which you can find any kind of stability and peace.[24]

It seems probable that the dryness Fox experienced in this ocean of darkness was akin to what Merton calls the "desert of aridity." This speaks powerfully to what Fox must have been going through in those searching years. At one level, Fox saw nothing, felt nothing and apprehended nothing. At another level, he felt negatively, like a stranger, alone; it was like melancholy, stuck in the deep. Merton's words about "interior suffering" and "anxiety" seem particularly descriptive.

Merton has stated that the experience of aridity can displace the Spirit by displacing one, i.e., putting one in the ocean of darkness. In fact, displacement is a technical, psychological term Gerald May uses to describe resisting spiritual experiences through a particular kind of defense.

> Displacement may well be the most common spiritual defense of our times. Here we seek to assuage our spiritual hunger through some physical, mental, or interpersonal activity that is not as threatening. Thus, we might seek to fill the void in our hearts by drinking, over-eating, or taking drugs. Or we may seek meaning through hard work, intense relationships, or powerful conquests rather than through the more self-abandoning paths of spiritual growth.[25]

Seeing how this typically works in contemporary society gives a clue how Fox may have been tempted by his own form of displacement. But Fox chose to go to the place of question rather than displace the question. One thing is clear. Fox did not displace his quest for God with alternatives to God. He chose the high road and he risked himself directly. He attended to his spiritual hunger, aware of the gnawing pangs to seek God. Fox would not settle for a pseudo-God (idol). Fox was a different model because he stayed on the path until God met him.

Fox employed characteristics of the ocean of darkness to describe other people. Fox talked about the dullness and sleepiness which portray a person immersed in the ocean of darkness.

> But I observed a dullness and drowsy heaviness upon people, which I wondered at, for sometimes when I would set myself to sleep, my mind went over all to the beginning, in that which is from everlasting to everlasting. I saw death was to pass over this sleepy, heavy state, and I told people they must come to witness death to that sleepy, heavy nature, and a cross to it in the power of God, that their minds and hearts might be on things above.[26]

This quotation obviously goes beyond other references used so far as Fox shared about his ministry to others. Indeed, it points to that means by which humans are opened out of the ocean of darkness. Nevertheless, it serves well here to give a fuller description of the ocean of darkness. That is the place where dullness, sleepiness and heaviness characterize one's life.

Because of these, the telling psychological/spiritual experience is a developing sense of *impotence* for the person to change. Feeling impotent, one really is "at sea," trapped and shut in one's own sleepiness, too heavy to do anything but sink, and to sink is to die— at least emotionally and spiritually. On land, heaviness turns quickness into plodding; in the water, heaviness turns swimming into sinking. To be heavy is to be weighed down, causing immobility, and in the ocean leads to death by drowning. As an image used in the Bible, heaviness is particularly associated with the yoke. But it also can be used in the same context Fox used it, namely, the heaviness of one's sin or alienation from God. Another lament,

Psalm 38, uses this image of heaviness. "There is no soundness in my flesh because of thy indignation; there is no health in my bones because of my sin. For my iniquities have gone over my head; they weigh like a burden too heavy for me." (Ps. 38:3-4)

The actual linking of heaviness with sleepiness as Fox had used in the phrase, "drowsy heaviness" is found in the scene at the garden of Gethsemane. Peter is proud that though others fall away, he never will fail Jesus. Jesus prays and returns to find all sleeping. He exhorts them to "watch and pray that you may not enter into temptation." (Mt. 26:41). A second time Jesus prays and again returns to find them sleeping, "for their eyes were heavy." (Mt. 26:43) The themes of heaviness and sleepiness are linked powerfully in the Gethsemane story. The men's eyes were heavy and they slept. In Fox's language, this drowsy heaviness renders one careless and immobile. One cannot watch, nor see with the eyes closed. Symbolically, this suggests the closing of the body by the shutting of the eyes. One is not "open." This is another way of saying in the ocean of darkness everyone is under all, shut up.

To be closed or asleep, then, leads to ignorance. Not to see, or to be asleep, makes one ignorant through inattention. Being asleep is an age-old spiritual image describing ignorance. Fox used the images of sleepiness, dullness and heaviness to describe the "condition" of humankind apart from God. This state of being describes a person who is not spiritually aware. This is what Fox meant by the ocean of darkness and death.

In this ocean of darkness there is no light by which to be "enlightened." It is as if the eyes were closed. It is functional blindness. This sleepy, heavy state so weighs the human spirit down that humans may never know another condition. What humans in this ocean of darkness "see," they assume is "normal." In this, they are truly pathological—sick, and do not even know it. This is the horror and, finally, tragedy of this condition: humans are sick and do not know it. It is this shift to the image of sickness—pathology—which enables one in the twentieth century to grasp what Fox in a pre-Freudian period described. To this pathological condition the current century offers therapy. In another century—the seventeenth—Fox experienced the grace of God to speak to this condition. In Fox's language, grace awakens and enlightens.

Through Fox's language of awakening, enlightening and opening, one realizes the ocean of darkness is not an absolute state of humanity. Rather, it is a particular, specific condition which can be and was for Fox, not only qualified, but overcome. This movement of overcoming is the subject of further chapters. It will suffice here in this section on the ocean of darkness to cite a lengthy text from the end of his despairing period. Here one can see Fox being brought out of the ocean of darkness.

> Then after this there did a pure fire appear in me; then I saw how he sat as a refiner's fire and as the fuller's soap; and then the spiritual discerning came into me, by which I did discern my own thought, groans and sighs, and what it was that did veil me, and what it was that did open me. And that which could not abide in the patience nor endure the fire, in the Light I found to be the groans of the flesh (that could not give up to the will of God), which had veiled me, and that could not be patient in all trials, troubles and anguishes and perplexities, and could not give up self to die by the Cross, the power of God, that the living and quickened might follow him; and that that which would cloud and veil from the presence of Christ, that which the sword of the Spirit cuts down and which must die, might not be kept alive. And I discerned the groans of the spirit which did open me, and made intercession to God, in which spirit is the true waiting upon God for the redemption of the body and of the whole creation. And by this true spirit, in which the true sighing is, I saw over the false sighings and groanings. And by this invisible spirit I discerned all the false hearing and the false seeing, and the false smelling which was atop, above the Spirit, quenching and grieving it; and that all they that were there were in confusion and deceit, where the false asking and praying is, in deceit, and atop in that nature and tongue that takes God's holy name in vain, and wallows in the Egyptian sea, and asketh but hath not. For they hate his light and resist the Holy Ghost, and turn the grace into wantonness, and rebel against the Spirit, and are erred from the faith they should ask in, and from the Spirit they should pray by...The divine light of Christ manifesteth all things...[27]

A constellation of images emerge in this passage to embellish the root metaphor, the ocean of darkness: false self, veil, confusion and deceit. Considering each of these culminates in a full comprehension of the reality Fox called the ocean of darkness.

The image of veil is functionally like the image of sleep. In its own way veil communicates the feeling of being shut up and under all. This passage from the *Journal* and, particularly the symbolism of veiling, shows the "before and after" sides of religious transformation. Opposite to the image of veiling is "opening," giving an even better feeling for understanding the "veiling" means being closed, concealed or shut in. In this passage Fox employed the term, veil, three times, as that which had come between himself and God. The veil, then, is that perception of reality which divides. As such, it separated Fox from the presence of God. In this condition of separation, Fox, at first was veiled from knowing the state in which he lived. That was the initial difficulty. It is, as if, a sleeping person needs to be awake in order to know they are sleeping!

Although Fox probably had a passage from Malachi in mind when writing about the pure fire which appeared in him after the veil was opened, the veiling/opening theme is articulated in the terminology drawn from the apostle Paul.[28] The veiling is related to the "flesh" as the opening is related to the "spirit."[29] Fox discovered that the "groans of the flesh" were those aspects of his self which did not know God and/or would not submit to the will of God. These groans "had veiled me," he confessed. That this part of his self had veiled him only points to the real difficulty: namely, most humans become so habituated in this "veiled" condition, it seems naturally preferable. This "self" establishes itself as god and is highly committed to itself—it becomes selfish!

This is the false self that must die if God is to be known and the true self be born. This false self exists in the ocean of darkness and chooses to remain there. This is the self which, as Fox eloquently stated, "could not give up self to die by the Cross, the power of God." This is the false self Fox encountered in the rending of his veil.

Although Fox did not extensively use the image of the false self to describe the alienated human from God, this image described his experience. Furthermore, the language of the false self is extensively used in contemporary spirituality. To understand the false self enables one to see why confusion and deceit are primary descriptions of the ocean of darkness.

Merton's description of the false self has briefly been cited.[30] Probably no contemporary writer on spirituality has been more eloquent on the false/true self than Merton. Merton keenly ties together the false self and illusion.

Every one of us is shadowed by an illusory person: a false self. This is the man that I want myself to be but who cannot exist, because God does not know anything about him. And to be unknown of God is altogether too much privacy. My false and private self is the one who wants to exist outside the reach of God's will and God's love—outside of reality and outside of life. And such a self cannot help but be an illusion.[31]

The false self who exists—as it understands itself—beyond the reach of God's will and love seems very close to that self Fox described which refused to give itself up to the cross. Keying this refusal is the illusion which motivates and perpetuates the false self.

Using this paradox, Alan Jones pursues the notion of illusion and how it is linked to the false self. The process of beginning to understand the illusions about our "self" is the process of dying. Jones writes:

This "death of the self" comes when we realize that the impression that we possess persisting and permanent souls or selves is an illusion. What does such a "dying" accomplish? For one thing, it pushes the believer more and more deeply into the desert. It invites the believer to sit loosely to his or her "self." In fact, it challenges the believer to *dis*believe in the self as an abiding entity.[32]

In one real sense this quotation from Jones goes too far too fast. He talks about "the believer" and the "death of the self." In the ocean of darkness one is not yet aware of being a believer nor has one experienced the "death of self," even though the "self" may be feeling as if dead or threatened.

In fact, what characterizes the ocean of darkness is living under the illusion that the "false self" is real; one accepts and lives out the illusions as if it were both real and true. Dramatically, in the ocean of darkness people live out their days ignorantly and hypnotically! So the Jones' quotation goes too far—but one has to be that far in order "to see" and, then, back up to the illusion to expose it for what it is. Standing with Jones and the believer at this point of seeing is to stand at the place of transformation. It is to be at the time of conversion when and where one knows change is happening.

Again, Merton's words are most instructive to explain the nature of this change. It is the unmasking of illusions as the false self is exposed with no assurance there is anything else! In speaking about the contemplative prayer of the monk Merton alleges that:

...the way of prayer brings us face to face with the sham and indignity of the false self that seeks to live for itself alone and to enjoy the "consolation of prayer" for its own sake. This "self" is pure illusion, and ultimately he who lives for and by such an illusion must end either in disgust or in madness.[33]

This quotation could refer to Fox's world or our contemporary world. To live out the false self ultimately ends in disgust or madness.

To be stuck in the ocean of darkness is to be in the place of death, and although one may be alive, one experiences this "dying" as disgust or madness. One feels alone and is driven madly toward relationships which often are not deep nor meaningful. One despairs and is re-captured by the illusions about self. One can feel dry and barren and look for ways to moisturize the soul. One is frequently sad and melancholy and seeks happy release through drugs or inappropriate emotional "uppers." One lives life sleep-walking, dull, sluggish, deep in this ocean. Even when there is intelligence, it frequently is not used wisely! All about one in this ocean is darkness, deceit and confusion. From a contemporary spirituality point of view, this summarizes the experience of the ocean of darkness. Fox's experience and language said something about human nature lived in separation and alienation from God. Fox is a powerful model because he chose to go on with the search. He chose to be opened, to become vulnerable, in order to be found by the hound of heaven. He was found and his ministry witnesses to his discovery. But on the way, he suffered the agony of putting to death the old self, and the ocean of darkness was penetrated by Christ's light to reveal the false self.

Fox felt it necessary to have a sense of all conditions in humankind. In effect, however, he discovered there are really only two conditions: this ocean of darkness and death, and then, the ocean of light and love. These two oceans or conditions were at the heart of Fox's spirituality and all of Christian spirituality. The ocean of darkness defines and describes the human predicament—humans grow up believing they are independent, free, and gods. The perversity of this condition of darkness is that it can look and feel so attractive! Fox chose to travel the road of authenticity rather than attractiveness. To choose to travel this spiritual road of authenticity rather than the social road of acceptability often spells trouble. Elfrida Vipont suggests both the cost and prize of Fox's choice.

George Fox was rapidly becoming a village problem. It seemed extraordinary for a good-looking, promising, clever young man to be unable to settle down. Some said the obvious thing was for him to get married, and doubtless they would have found a wife for him into the bargain if required. Others suggested army life as the very thing for a restless youth with no more sense than to go round asking questions about religion, at a time when the country was alternating between the violence and horror of civil war and the strains and stresses of an uneasy peace. Army life would make a man of him, they thought. George refused even to consider the idea. He needed something to make a man of him, he knew, but it must be a whole man and quite another kind of army; he needed somebody to show him how to put on the whole armour of God.[34]

II

BROKENNESS OF HEART

For I was very much altered in countenance and person as
if my body had been new moulded or changed. And while
I was in that condition, I had a sense and discerning given
me by the Lord, through which I saw plainly that when many
people talked of God and of Christ, etc., the Serpent spoke
in them; but this was hard to be borne. Yet the work of the
Lord went on in some, and my sorrows and troubles began
to wear off and tears of joy dropped from me, so that I could
have wept night and day with tears of joy to the Lord, in
humility and brokenness of heart. And I saw into that which
was without end and things which cannot be uttered, and of
the greatness and infiniteness of the love of God, which
cannot be expressed by words. For I had been brought
through the very ocean of darkness and death...[1]

The process of moving from the ocean of darkness and death to the
ocean of light and love passes necessarily through humility and
brokenness of heart. When sorrows and troubles begin to erode and
tears of joy replace these darkness experiences, one knows he or she
has crossed over and is making it. Fox was brought over to the other
side or, as he put it, was brought from the world's ways to discover
the Spirit's ways. This chapter examines the beginning of that process
focused in the ocean of darkness. What does one experience as she

or he thinks about those first workings of the Lord? What does one primarily feel as God initiates the call to individuals in the darkness? The beginning of this process frequently touches the characteristic false self in the ocean of darkness as the *illusion* which constructs the world of meaning by living out its existence in a false world. In a word, one has to die to this self in order for the true or authentic self to be born. This process characterizes the passage from the ocean of *darkness* to the ocean of *light*.

This dying to the false self is nothing more than acknowledging the illusions, the mythology, which construct the world of darkness for one's false self. The tricky part is in recognizing these illusions, the darkness may "look like" light! Alan Jones says that our 'dying,' then has to do with the stripping away of illusions."[2] Fox characterizes this dying to illusions as a beginning movement within the ocean of darkness—the beginning of questioning and the introduction of tension and anxiety. This is where Fox risked hearing and seeing that he was "living a lie," as Merton describes this process.

> But underlying all life is the ground of doubt and self-questioning which sooner or later must bring us face to face with the ultimate meaning of our life. This self-questioning can never be without a certain existential "dread"—a sense of insecurity, of "lostness," of exile, of sin. A sense that one has somehow been untrue not so much to abstract moral or social norms but to one's own inmost truth. "Dread" in this sense is not simply a childish fear of retribution, or a naive guilt, a fear of violating taboos. It is the profound awareness that one is capable of ultimate bad faith with himself and with others: that one is living a lie.[3]

This is the word to hear and the insight to be given for anyone to begin the movement out of the ocean of darkness and death.

That hearing and sight are key to removal from the ocean of darkness becomes clear through the experiences of Fox's, both in his conversion experience and, later, in his ministry. What this means is the reality of the ocean of darkness and death is always a present possibility waiting to be actualized. Even though one may be moved out of this ocean in a conversion or transformational experience, one can always, as Fox occasionally did, come back under the weight of this ocean. Hence, it is easy to understand why he employed the darkness and death language to describe his experience long after his conversion. In a account of his travels in the ministry in 1670, a rich passage illustrates this. Traveling in south-eastern England, Fox narrates:

...as I was going towards Rochester I lighted and walked down a hill; and a great weight and oppression fell on my spirit. So I got on my horse again, but my weight and oppression remained so as I was hardly able to ride. So we came to Rochester; but I was very weak to ride, and very much loaden and burdened with the world's spirits, so that my life was oppressed under them...So I endeavored to ride ten miles to Stratford, three miles off London...but I was exceedingly weak...at last I lost my hearing and sight so as I could not see nor hear. And I said unto Friends that I should be as a sign to such as would not see, and such as would not hear the Truth.[4]

Fox connected the weight and oppression of the world's spirits with the loss of his hearing and sight. In this instance it happened to him during the course of his ministry. What seems just as true is that this loss is the condition of any who are under the load and burden of the world's spirits.

The cause of this blindness and deafness is rooted in the very essence of the ocean of darkness, namely, humans in this condition are living in alienation from their God. From the heart of this separation from God ensues a commitment to idolatry, typically lived out as some form of selfishness. It is not the kind of idolatry which fashions golden calves (Exodus 32). Rather, it is apparently a much more benign idolatry, but idolatry nevertheless. It is idolatrous to set one's self up as a god, to live for one's "self," to misperceive or deny what is real and true; idolatry is to live this lie.

This kind of idolatry is typically perpetuated by illusions. At the heart is the illusion that one's "self" is free and autonomous, that this "self" is independent. Life lived from these assumptions is a lie; it is life lived in sin. Sin is separation from God, alienation from the source of one's being and the resource of one's life.

Sin, then, is the primary theological truth of life found in the ocean of darkness and death. To be in this ocean is to be in sin—alienated from God. Although contemporary Christians and Quakers differ widely in assessing of the meaningfulness of the concept of sin, it is unmistakable that Fox had a view of sin significant for his spirituality.

Many contemporary Quakers and Christians have either ignored or underestimated the function of sin in Fox's thought and experience. He certainly does not dwell upon it but the present purpose of outlining his spirituality notes the reality of sin. Sin is real because the ocean of darkness and death is real. One can do no better than highlight the most quoted passage from Fox's *Journal.*

> But as I had forsaken all the priests, so I left the separate preachers also, and those called the most experienced people; for I saw there was none among them all that could speak to my condition. And when all my hopes in them and in all men were gone, so that it had nothing outwardly to help me, nor could tell what to do, then, Oh then, I heard a voice which said, 'There is one, even Christ Jesus, that can speak to thy condition', and when I heard it my heart did leap for joy. Then the Lord did let me see why there was none upon the earth that could speak to my condition, namely, that I might give him all the glory; for all are concluded under sin, and shut up in unbelief as I had been...[5]

It is clear from this passage that Fox links the ocean of darkness and theological concept of sin. When Fox talked about his "condition," it referred to the ocean of darkness and death. Furthermore, the language of being "concluded under sin" is another way of talking about being caught in this ocean. In the last chapter, Fox spoke of being "shut up" in the ocean. Here that idea is comparable to being mired in unbelief. Sin, then, is the theological truth of life in this ocean of darkness.

It is not necessary to develop in detail a doctrine of sin, but it is helpful to have a sense of the scope of what sin as a condition meant for Fox. It is clear one cannot understand his doctrine of salvation without understanding the human condition which Jesus Christ as savior "answers." This understanding of sin as the "condition" of the ocean of darkness and death is a much broader comprehension of sin than the usual definition. This is particularly important dealing with a figure like Fox, who basically was not doing anything wrong or being bad in a moral sense and, in this way, could not be condemned as sinner. Yet, he felt very much in a condition of alienation and separation from God, shut up in the ocean of darkness, in sin.

Paul Tillich, among contemporary theologians, offers an understanding of sin as a "condition" rather than a moral "wrong" or "bad act." Tillich borrowed the terminology of "estragement," especially as it had developed in nineteenth century philosophical existentialism. Tillich began his analysis in terms appropriate to Fox by differentiating human *existence* and human *essence.* God created humans essentially good and pure. But sin altered this essential quality so that after Adam and Eve human existence is characteristically different from what God intended. In Tillich's language, "the state of existence is the state of estrangement. Man is estranged from the ground of his being, from other beings, and from himself. The transition from essence to existence results in personal guilt and universal tragedy."[6]

In language which could have been borrowed from Quaker tradition, Tillich develops this idea of estrangement.

> In estrangement, man is outside the divine center to which his own center essentially belongs. He is the center of himself and of his world. The possibility of leaving his essential center—and, with this possibility, the temptation— is given because structurally he is the only fully centered being.[7]

This language of separation from the center is another, contemporary metaphorical way of talking about entering or discovering that one is in the ocean of darkness. Alan Jones states that "we are free to become eccentric—that is off center."[8] One becomes eccentric when one becomes self-centered; and is tempted to be selfish. Selfishness is the condition of being self-centered, eccentric. This is sin.

The real problem here is that sin feels so normal! The illusion contends this is the way reality is supposed to be. Original sin is, then, this condition of estrangement which seems like the way it has always been. Any two year old child appears to be fully developed evidence of this. Sin of selfishness, as "normalcy," makes eccentric the one who chooses not to live sinfully! The eccentric appears to the world to be the one who apparently has been tempted to lose self rather than save self. In this sense, the spirituality of Fox is eccentric. This spirituality is a call to recognize blindness and deafness. It is a call to realize that the normalacy of selfishness is the ocean of darkness!

This is truly a tragic condition. Normally, in this condition one is, as it were, blind and deaf to the truth or reality of one's condition. The tragedy is that life in this ocean can look and feel acceptable, and even be at one level satisfying and temporarily meaningful! There is no urge for any other impetus, particularly when life and career have turned out to be successful and/or rewarding. Satisfying idolatry is so pernicious precisely because it is so subtle!

In his own way Merton points to this dimension of sin and suggests why the monk dares risk the satisfaction of such idolatry of "self."

> ...society itself, institutional life, organization, the "approved way," may in fact be encouraging us in the falsity and illusion. The deep root of monastic "dread" is the inner conflict which makes us guess that in order to be true to God and to ourselves we must break with the familiar, established and secure norms and go off into the unknown. "Unless a man hate father and mother." These words of Christ give some indication of the deep conflict which underlies all Christian conversion—the turning to a freedom based no longer on social approval and relative alienation, but on direct dependence on an invisible and inscrutable God, in pure faith.[9]

These words of Merton could not have been crafted more appropriately to describe Fox's experience had Merton known intimately this early Quaker. The key to the conversion journey is to be brought to the place of that inner conflict. It is only then that there is any suspicion that one truly is blind and deaf, that one has been and is in sin, that a lie is being lived!

The nature and course of that inner conflict, as Merton identifies it, begins the process of giving sight to the blind, hearing to the deaf and eccentricity to the "normal;" it is how one emerges from the ocean of darkness. In theological terms, people can emerge from the condition of sin, the state of Adam. As Fox declared in an epistle to Friends written in 1656:

> They who come to the church that is in God and Christ, must come out of the state that Adam is in, in the Fall, to know the state that he was in before he fell. And now they that live in the state that Adam is in, in the Fall, and who cannot believe of coming into the state he was in before he fell, come not to the Church of God, but are far from that, and are not passed from death to life, and likewise are enemies to the Cross of Christ, which is the power of God...For all the

poorness, emptiness, and barrenness is in the state that Adam is in, in the Fall, out of God's power.[10]

The conflict, as Fox demonstrated in his spiritual pilgrimage, is to become aware of the poorness, emptiness and barrenness of one's condition. Feeling conflictual, one stands at the threshold of change or through crisis one has already been thrust into change.

From a Franciscan Catholic perspective, Benedict Groeschel gives contemporary people a way of coming into the Spirit, a way which again sounds classically Quaker. Groeschel suggests that "most people undergo an *awakening*, i.e., one or a series of memorable experiences of the reality of the intangible. The experience may be consoling or threatening, or both...The awakening is also often an experience of light and darkness, of conflict and contract."[11] This quotation again points toward the bridge between the two oceans—the bridge which leads through conflict to resolution. But in this chapter the focus is on the emerging experience of the conflict rather than its resolution in the ocean of light.

Using this language of conflict, one normally refers to the first phase of the religious conversion process, the initial phase of questioning, tension, anxiety and stress.[12] There is probably no better way to understand the conflict which stands at the headwaters of this process of coversion than to focus on the feeling of anxiety. When Walter Conn speaks about moral conversion, he gives a splendid feeling and sense for what is at stake.

...the hard truth is that moral conversion is not easy; one does not just wake up one morning in a new moral world. Indeed, it is extremely difficult to overcome the resistance with which the psyche spontaneously responds to the possibility of conversion, of moving into a radically new horizon. For horizons define not abstractions but the concrete shape of one's living. And to contemplate a radical change in the style of concrete living that for many years has more or less successfully integrated the significant elements of one's personality—unconscious as well as conscious, practical as well as interpersonal—is, as Kierkegaard describes so vividly, to invite an experience of anxiety or dread.[13]

Seeing anxiety as the threshold of conflict can be the initial movement of God's Spirit in one's life or it can be the provocation dealing with questions of meaning in relation to God's Spirit.

It is in this latter sense that Gerald May notes anxiety's role. He observes that "many times I have seen people forced by anxiety to confront issues of meaning, consciousness, self, and God in ways that have led to deep spiritual openings, levels they would never have faced had they not been deeply distressed with their lives."[14] This certainly describes the journey Fox travelled when he began those four years of 1643-47 in the wilderness, tempted to despair. This anxiety characterized the uneasiness Fox felt about his "place" in the world and is not far from Tillich's existential anxiety.

Tillich moves straight to the spiritual aspect of the predicament when he says that "finitude in awareness is anxiety."[15] Because one is human, conscious and aware of who and what one is, one is aware of finitude—coming into existence and passing out of existence. Inevitably, to be aware of this produces anxiety. Philosophically, one can talk about the threat of non-being. In strict language it could be said, "we are scared to death, or of death!"

Tillich developed this notion of anxiety resulting from the knowledge one will die which he labels "ontological anxiety."

> Like finitude, anxiety is an ontological quality. It cannot be derived; it can only be seen and described. Occasions in which anxiety is aroused must be distinguished from anxiety itself. As an ontological quality, anxiety is as omnipresent as is finitude. Anxiety is independent of any special object which might produce it; it is dependent only on the threat of non being—which is identical with finitude. In this sense it has been said rightly that the object of anxiety is "nothingness."[16]

Profoundly, Tillich can finally note that "psychotherapy cannot remove ontological anxiety, because it cannot change the structure of finitude. But it can remove compulsory forms of anxiety and can reduce the frequency and intensity of fears. It can put anxiety 'in its proper place.'"[17]

Anxiety in its proper place recognizes the human predicament that death is certain. Additionally, there is no guarantee one will or can make sense out of this predicament, or make meaning out of one's life on the way to death. To engage this quest for meaning is to engage anxiety and not choose denial or pretension as coping mechanisms. Fox chose to do this as his initial words in the *Journal* exemplify, "that all may know the dealings of the Lord with me, and the various exercises, trials, and troubles though which he led me in order to prepare and fit me for the work into which he had appointed me."[18] This quickly led Fox to know his condition which caused anxiety in the face of despair. For this he needed spiritual direction, not psychotherapy.

Thomas Merton describes why anxiety at the first blush of conflict leads so progressively to the temptation to despair and then to despair itself.

> Despair is the absolute extreme of self-love. It is reached when a man deliberately turns his back on all help from anyone else in order to taste the rotten luxury of knowing himself to be lost. In every man there is hidden some root of despair because in every man there is pride that vegetates and springs weeds and rank flowers of self-pity as soon as our own resources fail us. But because our own resources inevitably fail us, we are all more or less subject to discouragement and to despair.[19]

Merton analyzes despair as the final human decision to declare itself to be lost—helpless and hopeless. Anxiety is the emergence of this possibility to decide for despair. Fear, as psychologically experienced anxiety, is the first inner rumblings of one's aloneness and absolute isolation.

At this point it is well to return to the language describing Fox. What is remarkable is the consistently encountered expression that he was "tempted to despair." Fox did not employ the existential language of anxiety. Instead, he spoke more classically of temptations. It seems clear, however, that in this period of temptation to despair (1643-47), the language of temptations was synonymous with anxiety. For Fox, then, his world of temptations was his world of conflict which he engaged and embraced rather than avoiding or running from it.

Engaging the conflict seems to be the first choice given to any person. This was where Fox clearly seized the initiative to wrestle with those temptations which assailed him. He attested to this when he wrote during that period of near-despair about life in his twentieth year (1644).

But temptations grew more and more and I was tempted almost to despair, and when Satan could not effect his design upon me that way, then he laid snares for me and baits to draw me to commit some sin, whereby he might take advantage to bring me to despair. I was about twenty years of age when these exercises came upon me, and some years I continued in that condition, in great trouble...[20]

This incident recounts a time during that first year after Fox broke off relations with family and friends (September, 1643) and began his four year seeking. Noteworthy was his sense that the temptations increased. Indeed, that they "grew more and more" conveys a sense of multiplication in a kind of geometrical compounding. One has the feeling from Fox that it came to be overwhelming. Things, even life, were experienced as out of control.

At this point he was willing to look for help. Following the passage just cited, Fox tells the reader:

...from Barnet I went to London, where I took a lodging, and was under great misery and trouble there, for I looked upon the great professors of the city of London, and I saw all was dark and under the chain of darkness.[21]

It is sad to hear Fox describe his own condition as "under great misery and trouble" and, yet, realize those in darkness were not going to be able to share any light. He received advice, but no direction. His family wanted him to get married; he wanted wisdom. Others wanted him to join the army; he refused.[22] A contemporary observer has noted this inability to distinguish advice from direction.

Five pastors had a turn at providing spiritual direction for George Fox in the first months of his religious awakening. Each of them failed badly. Fox was in his late adolescence when he ran into this discouraging sequence of spiritual misdirections...That the five did badly is not surprising. George Fox was complex. Spiritual direction is difficult. Pastoral wisdom is not available on prescription. Every person who comes to a pastor with a heart full of shapeless longings and a head full of badgering questions is complex in a new way. There are not fail-proof formulae.[23]

Even though Fox did not receive direction from family and priests, he did find himself directed. By engaging these temptations to despair, Fox walked into the arena where he met the director in person, Christ Jesus. Fox did not receive from people helpful direction, but poor advice. The question is, "what would a good spiritual director have told him?" Martin Thornton, a contemporary Anglican writer, shares where he would begin with Fox, or, where Fox probably began as he became aware of the temptations growing "more and more." Thornton says that:

> The beginner is not necessarily a vicious sinner to be purged, neither is he without gifts and graces; he is a flux of potentiality, and the most obvious thing about him is that his spiritual potential is unresolved by order and choice: he is in a muddle. His first need is for *regula*, system, to be worked out with the utmost care in accordance with *attrait*, remembering always that *regula*—Rule—is diametrically opposite to a list of little rules.[24]

Indeed, Fox was in a muddle. Perhaps, it is even worse than a muddle as Fox struggled with the temptations toward despair. For Fox, giving into this despair would be the ultimate sin—to be finally separated from God. In this sense, the Pauline dictum that "the wages of sin is death," becomes understandable. (Rom. 6:23)

For Fox, to commit sin, to give way to temptation, was to choose death. For him "death" was experienced not physically, but emotionally and cognitively as despair. It was to live in the world "as if dead, living in deadness." Fox's temptations to despair, then, were more than a thrust at lust, tobacco or drink; it was flirting with death itself! Faced with this, many people do not even choose to begin the spiritual journey. Rather, they choose to remain in the muddle of their own creation! Sin is the primary theological truth of life in the ocean of darkness.

The first phase of this wrestling often feels conflictual. Fox wrote about that fleshly part (the not-God part of the human person) which "had veiled me...and could not give up self to die by the Cross, the power of God."[25] Fox took up this Pauline language and pointed further to the theological nature of this inner conflict when he said in the midst of a vision in the year 1647:

> The law of the Spirit crosseth the fleshly mind, spirit and will, which lives in disobedience, and doth not keep within the law of the Spirit. I saw this law was the pure love of God which was upon me, and which I must go through, though I was troubled while I was under it; for I could not be dead to the law but through the law which did judge and condemn that which is to be condemned...[26]

Fox was troubled while under the working of the law of the Spirit. This indicated the working of the conflict in his awakening to the ocean of darkness.

For Fox this conflict was described as a struggle between two wills: the earthly, fleshly will and God's will. It is a struggle between the false self and the possibility of an emerging, true self. Fox recognized human will to be "the selfish, fleshly, earthly will which reigns in its own knowledge and understanding, that must perish, and in its wisdom, that is devilish."[27] This selfish, fleshly, earthly will exercises its own desires and direction, leading one into temptation and holding one in sin. This power creates separation from God and fashions, as it were, one's own ocean of darkness. From this idolatry to self begins the separation from the source of life itself and the choice of deadness, deadness which finally results in death itself.

The problem is that so often this selfish, earthly will seems like the only "person" one knows. It is taken for one's real self; in fact, it is *real*, but is one's false self. The real, *authentic* self can only be known by seeing the real, false self put to death. Most people are well-defended against coming to know the truth of their sinful condition, the ocean of darkness. They prefer to ignore or deny truth: that they are a false self. In the words of Henri Nouwen in this beginning struggle "the danger is real. It is the danger of living the whole of our life as one long defense against the truth of our condition, one restless effort to convince ourselves of our virtuousness."[28] Nouwen is just as clear as Merton and countless others throughout the centuries: as God begins to call one, this wrestling with the truth of one's false self is a *struggle*. "It is the struggle to die to the false self. But this struggle is far, far beyond our own strength. Anyone who wants to fight his demons with his own strength, is a fool."[29]

Being able to fight demons means one is already on the way. More predictably, the initial response is to ignore or deny that the self seen is one's false self. For too many people, this continues through a lifetime! But for others like Fox, one "takes up" the struggle—risking the false self as perhaps (and likely) the only self one ever knew. Often people resent dealing with the fact that, as real as they might be, they are, nevertheless, not really authentic! There is a way by which this struggle unfolds. Watching how Fox did it charts the way to use classical spiritual direction phrases.

The initial phase is the "preconversion"[30] phase, using the language from Bailey Gillespie, which includes the conflictual condition of questioning, tension, anxiety and stress. To engage this conflict and to risk death to the false self and birth of the authentic self usually involves a two step process: renunciation and detachment. This is what Fox did in September, 1643, when he broke relations with family and friends. To make the break was to "take up" the struggle, to embrace the conflict.

This two step process of renunciation and detachemnt is classically the means by which the Christian church has understood Jesus' words as a call to discipleship. "If any man would come after me, let him deny himself and take up his cross and follow me. For whoever would save his life will lose it; and whoever loses his life for my sake and the gospel's will save it." (Mark 8:34-35) This is the Christian key to life which Fox "went for" and from which so many of his contemporaries and our contemporaries run. Merton points to the irony of chosing to perpetuate one's false self in deadness by refusing to take the two steps of renunciation and detachment.

> It is the easiest thing in the world to possess this life (divine, authentic) and this joy; all you have to do is believe and love; and yet people waste their whole lives in appalling labor and difficulty and sacrifice to get things that make real life impossible.
> This is one of the chief contradictions that sin has brought into our souls; we have to do violence to ourselves to keep from laboring uselessly for what is bitter and without joy, and we have to compel ourselves to take what is easy and full of happiness as though it were against our interests, because for us the line of least resistance leads in the way of greatest hardship and sometimes for us to do what is, in itself, most easy, can be the hardest thing in the world.[31]

Fox chose the hardest thing in the world. By breaking relationships, he began to renounce his false self and to detach himself from his inauthentic self.

Seventh century Greek theologican, John Climacus, wrote the most widely used handbook on ascetic life in the Greek Orthodox church. Although Fox was not a monk, nor are most people who respond to God's call, nevertheless, the words of Climacus help all to understand this initial phase of renunciation and detachment. In his first step, the renunciation of life, Climacus has some unfortunate anti-body assumptions, but, nevertheless, has a clear sense of the process of detachment from "the world." Climacus begins by affirming that "God is the life of all free beings."[32] Humans will never know this God—and authentic life—so long as they are attached to the world and their "self" as a creature of this world. Climacus suggests the prize of life is received when they "willingly turn from the things of this life, either for the sake of the coming kingdom, or because of the number of their sins, or on account of their love of God."[33]

Renunciation is the process of disengaging from the world as humans know it, life as they routinely live it, and then, beginning to look for and seek out the God who is creator of a new world and redemptive life as they might live it. Without this kind of disengagement or renunciation, the spiritual path is likely not to be discovered. The imagery of dying characterizes the move from the false self to the authentic self. The one who turns away from the world, Climacus says:

> ...should imitate those who sit by the tombs outside the city. Let him not disist from ardent raging tears, from the wordless moan of the heart, until he sees Jesus Himself coming to roll back the rock of hardness off him, to free the mind, that Lazarus of ours, from the bonds of sin, to say to His ministering angels, "Loose him from his passions and let him go to blessed dispassion."[34]

Climacus prefers dispassion in a way that many in the twentieth century might be uncomfortable, but he is not against passion as a zeal for God. Indeed, by the process of renouncing commitment to the world, individuals will be free to live and love God and through their passionate relationship to appropriately love the world. In fact, this love of God becomes the driving force towards renunciation.

> The man who renounces the world because of fear is like burning incense, which begins with fragrance and ends in

smoke. The man who leaves the world in hopes of a reward is like the millstone that always turns around on the same axis. But the man who leaves the world for the love of God has taken fire from the start, and like fire to set fuel, it soon creates a conflagration.[35]

Climacus addressed not only his time, but also seventeenth century English life or twentieth century American life. So many people live life, but not passionately, without any fire.

To live life dispassionately is like living in Egypt. In the biblical sense, to be in Egypt is to have freedom of movement, but to be a prisoner. To be in Egypt is to be able to move about but unable to go anywhere! In that sense movement is mere illusion if one thinks one is going somewhere.

The first thing required is the discovery that one's Egypt is bondage and bondage is the ocean of darkness and death. Fox knew this experientially when he talked about being brought through that ocean of darkness. In the quotation with which this chapter began Fox continued:

Even through that darkness was I brought, which covered-over all the world, and which chained down all, and shut up all in the death...Then could I say I had been in spiritual Babylon, Sodom, Egypt, and the grave...[36]

To be brought through the darkness involves the recognition and realization that one is in the darkness, that darkness has become one's "natural condition." Even recognizing the love of darkness and attachment to it, one can love the darkness to death!

To be brought through the darkness, Fox eloquently suggested, means facing one's darkness. One must face it, renounce it and detach from it. Renuciation of that which one loves in a warped way enables one to love in God's way. Many resent the advised words of Alan Jones when he declares:

Learning to love is learning to renounce the other for the sake of the other. We struggle daily with people who understand love only in terms of possession. To bring them and us through the thick wood of transference to the renunciation of love for the sake of love is one way of describing the task.[37]

There is a very clear link between this process of renunciation and learning to love. One learns this kind of love only by learning something about who one really is, discovering the nature of the false self and surrendering it up to be given a new, true self. In an ironic way, one learns how to be a lover by grappling with one's self in its naked, alone conditon. Only by learning who and what one is by oneself can one be authentically related to others.

Even if humans are relationally determined beings, they need to come to know themselves in their primary relationship with God before they become authentic lovers in God's world. In spiritual language, people, like Jesus, must go the wilderness, enter the desert, and be tested. This process of renunciation and detachment invariably takes them to the desert to recognize that their conditon is darkness.

In the Bible the renunciation/detachment phase of the spriitual life is exemplified by the wilderness sojourn of Jesus (Mark 1:12-13 and parallels). Rosemary Haughton characterizes this leading into the wilderness as a time requiring "the experience of utter loneliness."[38] Haughton goes on to characterize this "place" for Jesus and our need to go to be there also.

> It was necessary that he should penetrate, at this early stage of his mission, to the roots of life where the deeper exchanges take place, where human passion embraces and is embraced by God in the joy of differentiated love. But this is also the place where the power of evil—that is, of perverted exchange—is strongest...[39]

The desert place is where people encounter their evil and the world's evil. It is the place where, naked and alone, they wrestle with their own demons. It is where they recognize that their condition is like a swimmer in the ocean of darkness, that they are free to move around, but only like a fish and not a swimmer, always enslaved to the bondage of that medium.

This sense of bondage—or even fear—keeps most people committed to swim in the ocean of darkness. At least, it is movement and they pretend that they are getting some place! They can get rich or famous or whatever. They resent what renunciation asks: that they open their eyes and see the darkness. Thomas Metrton describes the modern spiritual pilgrimage as one in which people will even finally be asked to renounce resentment!

The most difficult and the most necessary of renunciations: to give up resentment. This is almost impossible, for without resentment modern life would probably cease to be human at all. Resentment enables us to survive the absurdity of existence in a modern city. It is the last-ditch stand of freedom in the midst of confusion. The confusion is inescapable, but at least we can refuse to accept it, we can say "No." We can live in a state of mute protest.

But, if resentment is a device which enables man to survive, it does not enable him, necessarily, to survive healthily. It is not a real exercise of freedom. It is not a genuine expression of personal integrity. It is the mute, animal protest of a mistreated psychophysical organism. Driven too far it becomes mental sickness; that too, is an "adaptation" in its own way. But it is an adaptation by way of escape.[40]

To renounce resentment of the world, and even, of the self stuck in our world brings one to the wilderness. It allows one to begin to disengage and to unhook from those sinful hooks and despairing engagements. To renounce resentment risks giving up the only power one feels is left: to hate. If one can not love and hate, then maybe the nothingness of despair is it. This literally scares one to death! But as the song, *The Rose*, says, it is "the soul afraid of dying that never learns to live."[41]

The wilderness is where one risks death in order to live, risking companionship instead of loneliness, love instead of resentment. Jesus is the model and guide. Rosemary Houghton charts it this way.

In that wilderness, isolated from the past, from other people, from everyday consciousness, Jesus entered willingly and urgently into a loneliness so absolute that only two things could touch it: love, and rejection of love. Loneliness and temptation go together, and if you want to encounter temptation pure, then the desert in some form or other is the place you have to go, which is, of course, why most of us avoid it like the devil.[42]

Clearly, one sees this description of the wilderness as similar to the ocean of darkness Fox experienced and described. Fox did not balk; he walked into the face of temptation and was anxious about despairing. Only then was he able to experience spiritual detachment from his world. In the words of Haughton, he was touched by God's love. In Fox's words in the opening of this chapter, he saw "the greatness and infiniteness of the love of God."

To be brought to this place meant Fox fought the demons of fear and anxiety, overcoming the devil of temptation and despair. As Climacus says:

> There are demons to assail us after our renunciation of the world. They make us envy those who remain on the outside and who are merciful and compassionate...Their hostile aim is to bring us by way of false humility either to turn back to the world or...to plunge down the cliffs of despair.[43]

Climacus states the choice well: detachment or despair. To return to the world will ultimately lead to despair. Fox talked about being *tempted* to despair, but never despairing. Yet, he was able through detachmet to dis-engage from the world, to learn love and to re-engage in a minsitry of love. In a word, he became an exile.

He became an exile from his Egypt, travelled through the wilderness of detachment and knew and lived in the condition of joy and peace which Jesus called the kingdom. He understood how detachment from the world enabled his exodus from the ocean of darkness and provided the breakthrough to the ocean of light and love.

The pithy saying of John Climacus characterizes this process; "Detachment is good and its mother is exile."[44] He continues with the admonition: "Run from Egypt, run and do not turn back. The heart yearning for the land there will never see Jerusalem..."[45] Detachment is given birth by exile, by the choice to leave Egypt and go into the wilderness, heading for Jerusalem. Detachment is good; the kingdom is better, yet one never gets to the better without going through the good. Detachment is the backing away from ones' world and one's "self" in order to see in a new way and from a new place. The initial place and perspective is exile. Exile, hopefully, will be both transitory and temporary—on the way to the kingdom. But, one notes carefully this terrain because it is not a just-once-visited-place!

Climacus described the place of exile in clarion terms. He declared that it is:

> ...an irrevocable renunciation of everything in one's familiar

surrounding that hinders one from attaining the ideal of holiness. Exile is a disciplined heart, unheralded wisdom, an unpublicized understanding, a hidden life, masked ideals. It is unseen meditation, the striving to be humble, a wish for poverty, the longing for what is divine. It is an outpouring of love, a denial of vain glory, a depth of silence.[46]

As Climacus developed this idea, it is as if he had Fox in mind. Climacus declared that "exile is a separation from everything, in order that one may hold on totally to God. It is a chosen route of great grief. An exile is a fugitive, running from all relationships with his own relatives and with strangers."[47] In his exile, his four years of being on the run, tempted almost to despair, Fox made himself vulnerable to the God who was always and finally there for him. Vulnerability is availability. Merton says the "*Alleluia* is the song of the desert."[48] In order to hear and sing that alleluia, Fox would have to experience a breakthrough. Fox would have to learn how to sing!

Fox had already commenced the conversion process by walking into the risk of death to his "self." In order to experience breakthrough he exposed himself fully, without reservation. Fox ventured on the path of holiness. To be holy is to be set apart, to be called out—out of the world and out of one's self. The call to be holy begins with the call to be vulnerable. As Nouwen puts it, "our identity, our sense of self, is at stake. Secularity is a way of being dependent on the responses of our milieu."[49] Fox renounced his milieu. By detaching himself from its hold, he began the journey of exile to holiness. God broke through to lead him.

Rosemary Haughton, in her book, *The Passionate God*, uses the language of "breakthrough" to describe the action of the passionate God in the world. Although her focus is on the incarnation, it can more widely describe how people come to the authentic life, as Merton describes it and as Fox lived it, which requires a breakthrough, a conversion. For Haughton, it is Christianity, in the person of Jesus Christ, which is crucial. She declares that "people 'discover' that Chrsitianity is true by a conversion experience, in which they perceive, very simply and directly and without argument, that the revelation of God in Christ is what life is all about."[50]

Discovering what life is all about requires breaking away from the ocean of darkness and then realizing there is an ocean of light which is life. Haughton traces the contours of this breakthrough of God's passion in human hearts.

> The response to this recognition is passion: the thrust of the whole personality towards the strange 'home' it perceives. It is accompanied by intense emotion, which varies in quality according to the temperament from a gentle but strong and certain joy to a desperate violence which is afraid of losing that which is perceived. But something very odd precedes this: I can only describe it as a kind of 'gap', in which there is no feeling or 'movement' but a timeless instant of oneness. It is an experience of recognition so complete and profound that it is impossible to say what is recognized. That is why it is experienced as a 'gap', and it can be so contentless that the person recoils and takes refuge behind a hastily closed door. Passion, therefore, is the thrust which leaps that void; it is a leap of faith, without guarantees or even knowledge...[51]

This language of passion and of the passionate breakthrough is eminently useful to describe Fox's experience on the eve of his birth out of the ocean of darkness and death.

The gap which Haughton uncovered and described as the "timeless instant of oneness" could well be the theme of the next chapter. Fox used different language, but the experiences is characterized by Haughton's words. In order to beat that gap, there is that instant of oneness when one is brought back to the beginning. The gap is where the heart is broken and from the broken heart comes joy.

A breakthrough comes to those whose hearts have already been broken or whose hearts will break. The old self dies before the new self is born. At the beginning of this chapter Fox talked about the trouble and sorrows he bore. Those began to wear off and he was given tears of joy, joy measured by humility and felt by a heart made tender. The spirit and will of the old self had to be broken, not in the sense of "tamed," but literally broken, to "break-off," be separated away. It was not tamed in the sense of being brought under control or made nice. No, often there is a call to the kind of violence which can characterize birth, even in re-birth. The mother is exile and the breaking-off is the leaving of Egypt.

This break-off comes as result of that call to learn how to live. It is the restless, anxious awakening to the aimlessness of the ocean of darkenss. Haughton describes the breakthrough as a "self-giving toward a wholeness intensely desired."[52] Without the initial impulse of the breakthrough, people are reticent to self-giving, and are more concerned with self-preserving. It is truly love and love alone which calls for a giving of self. Without the breakthrough, there will not be an authentic self to love or to offer in love. So, the breakthrough initially calls for that self-giving to be a "giving up."

People are called to give up family and friends, illusions and pretensions of their "self." They are called to die to that self and risk knowing about resurrection. Fox declared time and time again that the ocean is one of darkness and death. In the call of God, experienced as passionate breakthrough, people are called to die to death!

The problem is becoming enamoured by darkness and death. Fox's breakthrough brought death to this ocean of darkness and death, and passed him over into another ocean, an ocean of light and love. He learned how to desire this death in order to be given authentic life and genuine love. In breaking off from the world's ways, Fox was given a new world! From the desert he was brought to a mountain and his heart leaped for joy.

40

III

MY HEART DID LEAP FOR JOY

And when all my hopes in them and in all men were gone,
so that I had nothing outwardly to help me, nor could tell
what to do, then, Oh then, I heard a voice which said, 'there
is one, even Christ Jesus, that can speak to thy condition', and
when I heard it my heart did leap for joy.[1]

These words from George Fox probably are the best-known and
most frequently quoted from his *Journal.* The first two chapters of
this book charted the human predicament as Fox personally experienced it; now Fox's words in summary fashion proclaim the divine
solution: Christ Jesus speaks to the human condition!

To understand what Fox meant by these words, one needs some
sense of the "condition" of the ocean of darkness and death to which
Christ Jesus speaks. From that state of darkness one is brought into
the light which both is Christ Jesus and is from him; brought from
the state of death into life and finally delivered into eternal life. From
separation into an encounter and relationship with Christ Jesus, one
is brought into union with the godhead itself. This passage proclaims
the centrality of Christ Jesus, or christology, to George Fox's spirituality .

This book does not develop Fox's christology, the doctrine of
Jesus as the Christ, in its full theological/philosophical sense. Rather,

it traces the role christology plays in Fox's experience of God coming to him as Christ Jesus who spoke to his condition. Alan Jones has defined spirituality as "the act of making connections."[2] Looking carefully both at how Fox experienced and talked about this "addressing" activity of Christ Jesus will show how Christ Jesus is the means by which God and humanity connect — or, as the case may be, re-connect. Christology is important, not only as a doctrine, but as the art of forming and sustaining connections.

The language of God through Christ Jesus "addressing" Fox's condition is used in order to avoid loaded terms. Words like salvation, redemption and born again may be appropriate for Fox's spirituality, but care is undertaken at the outset in making assumptions. To understand Christ Jesus "addressing" Fox's condition uses a neutral, non-theological term, but one which fits the context. Fox said that Christ Jesus could "speak" to his condition. And when he "heard" it, his heart did leap for joy.

Moving directly into the language Fox used to describe his experience of Christ Jesus speaking to his condition, comes the realization of how sensual that language is. Using the classifications of spirituality, Fox's particular mode of being spiritual is predominantly "affective." Martin Thornton, a contemporary British writer on spirituality, suggests that affective spirituality is more emotional and less intellectual, more spontaneous and less formal, more love-emphatic and less duty-oriented.[3] Detailing Fox's spirituality (and, some might argue, Quakerism in general), one sees that affective spirituality is more appropriate than its counterpart, the "speculative."[4] Indeed, there probably is no better clue to Fox's affective spirituality than the words of his response to Christ Jesus' address, "my heart did leap for joy," because the heart is central to affective spirituality.

To follow the heart of Fox is to follow the language of the heart. Even though he used words, they were words of the heart. Although not poetic, his language of the heart was imaginative and sensual, rich in symbols and metaphor. Fox's language tended to be more metaphorical than conceptual. Although language is an attempt to discover and convey meaning, metaphorical language is literal language suggesting another level of reality, inviting one to "perceive" what one sees. One must understand this operation before understanding what Fox might mean when he feels that Christ Jesus could speak to his condition. In what way did Christ speak, literally and metaphorically?

Sallie McFague tells us that "the response to a metaphor is similar to the response to a riddle: one 'gets' it or one does not, and what one 'gets' is the new, extended meaning..."[5] McFague continues by quoting Nelson Goodman when he says that "metaphor, it seems, is a matter of teaching an old word new tricks - of applying an old label in a new way."[6] All this suggests one will be led to feel and to think about the reality Fox describes to "get" his meaning. To "get" it does more than interest; it excites.

One final preliminary observation is that Christ Jesus addressing Fox's condition brings about the full "conversion" of George Fox. In the last chapter, V. Bailey Gillespie stated that there are three parts to the conversion process. That chapter looked closely at the pre-conversion stage, a stage involving the questioning, tension, anxiety and stress of the beginnings of a religious awakening.

In Gillespie's analysis this initial stage is followed by *crisis* and, then, *postconversion*. The opening quotation from Fox adroitly connects both of these stages into one movement. Gillespie characterizes the crisis of conversion as the point of the religious awakening process where there is a "sense of a greater presence, higher control, and self-surrender."[7] The postconversion stage Gillespie describes as that place where "relief, release, assurance, harmony, peace, ecstatic happiness," occurs.[8] In Fox's experience, the crisis stage was reached when he declared that all his hopes in the priests, the separate preachers and "the most experienced people" were gone. This invited and provoked crisis because it implied Fox would be stuck in the ocean of darkness; there would be nothing but despair and its spiritual mate, death.

At this point of crisis, one can best understand Fox's experience as conversion or transformation. Too often conversion is associated solely with a "born again" experience in a fundamentalist perspective. However, this definition is too limiting and superficial. Walter Conn uncovers the depth and profundity of the conversion experience when he distinguishes between conversion as *content* and as *structure.* He states "conversion is commonly understood as a change in the *content* of a person's faith or fundamental orientation."[9] The content is significant, but perhaps more crucial to understanding conversion is to describe the *structure* of the conversion process. Influenced by structural theories of development, Conn states "conversion is viewed from the perspective of structure rather than content, and may be understood as a *vertical* conversion: radically new questions creatively restructuring content (old or new) into a totally new horizon."[10]

Fox's experience, described in this chapter's initial quotation, depicted what happened as a structural change. The theologically expressed *content* of his faith changed less than the structure of his relationship to the God in whom he had faith. Citing the work and influence of Bernard Lonergan, Conn suggests the structural change characterizes conversion and, thus, an interpretative clue for Fox is that conversion is a falling-in-love.

> Lonergan's notion of religious conversion is both profound and powerful. For him religious conversion, like affective conversion, is a falling-in-love that establishes a person as a dynamic principle of benevolence and beneficence. But in religious conversion, one falls-in-love with God, one is grasped by ultimate concern. Being-in-love with God is 'total and permanent self-surrender without conditions, qualifications, reservations.' Religious conversion transforms a person into a 'subject in love, a subject held, grasped, possessed, owned through a total and so an other-worldly love.'[11]

Precisely at this point, the transforming address of Christ Jesus was heard as an invitation to relationship. Fox was moved to the joyful knowledge of the postconversion stage. He would never look back because he would never be the same. He had become, in the words of William James, a religious genius.

Having Christ Jesus speak to his condition so transformed Fox that he began to live out of a new place as a new person. His heart leaped for joy and his life spread love. Walter Conn describes well what this kind of authentic transformation means.

> In genuine Christian conversion, then, one does not simply learn a new doctrine about life or love (content), but through the life and love of Jesus one begins to understand the paradoxical truth that life is love, that the only truly self-fulfilling life is the life given up — even to death — in loving one's neighbor; through a relationship with God in Jesus one begins to embrace this truth; and through the following of Jesus one begins to live this truth.[12]

In the conversion process Fox was turned from himself to Christ himself, and discovered not only that Christ Jesus spoke to his condition, but something about the one who spoke. Fox used a classical, yet distinctive language to describe the process of responding to Christ Jesus' word. The beginning is described by Fox as a process of "turning." In theological language, the saving activity of the christological encounter turned Fox from himself (death) to the divinity itself (life). Central to this "saving" activity is the work of Christ Jesus (christology). This, however, is not simply, or even initially, a doctrinal assent; rather it is an experiential realization or awakening. Christ Jesus speaking to Fox's condition was not, first of all, a theological statement. Rather, it was an experiential transformation. As Fox repeatedly acknowledged, he was to *turn* people to Christ, that Light Within.

The Quaker language of "turning" is actually traditional conversion language. It is appropriate English usage for the Greek word, *metanoia*, which is typically translated "to turn around" or "to repent." Actually, "repent" is a rather weak translation for *metanoia* because repentance language does not powerfully enough include this sense of turning around, of re-orientation and re-directing. When Fox appropriates and applies the language of "turning," he was speaking from the biblical tradition of *metanoia.*

The language of *metanoia* gives a sense of the tradition from which Fox worked, because for him the Bible was fundamentally formative. The central conversion passage applied to the message of Jesus is Mark 1:14-15 and parallels. After being in the wilderness forty days following his baptism, Jesus began his ministry by "preaching the gospel of God, and saying, 'the time is fulfilled, and the kingdom of God is at hand; repent, and believe in the gospel.'" (Mark 1:14-15) The *metanoia*, the repenting or turning, comes because of Jesus' presence and challenge of the kingdom. The gospel of God proclaimed and, in an authentic way, incarnated by Jesus is the kingdom—the presence of God's realm or condition in the world. The saving activity of Jesus is the presentation and re-presentation of this kingdom in our world. Our response is to turn to this Christ, embrace his work and enter his kingdom. In Fox's language, this turning is our responding.

Also using the language of *metanoia* and turning is Acts 26:20, a speech by Paul before King Agrippa. Paul was sharing why he was engaged in his ministry of making disciples as a result of his vision on the way to Damascus. Paul said that he "declared first to those at Damascus, then at Jerusalem and throughout all the country of Judea, and also to the Gentiles, that they should repent and turn to God and perform deeds worthy of their repentance." In this passage Paul distinguishes *repentance* and *turning* but, in fact, both are really part of that reorientation process of living for God and not for self. What makes this a powerfully connecting passage to Fox is because Paul's own sense of *who he is* and *what his mission is* comes as a result of his vision of the Lord. This is comparable to Fox's experience of hearing a voice tell him that "there is one, even Christ Jesus, that can speak to thy condition."

Interestingly, when one looks closely at Fox's language, one realizes Fox does not use the language of "turning" for himself but uses it copiously to describe his ministry for others. The absence of turning language to describe his own conversion should not be misleading, however. In fact, the prior four year despair period is fundamentally a period of turning. The turning is nothing more than preparation, the re-orientation so that he might "see" and "hear." In Fox's case, he heard that voice speak to him, and was enabled to see.

Fox's turning literally put him in a place where he was opened up afresh to see and to hear Christ . Actually, the conversion language Fox preferred to describe his own experience is the language of "opening," which emerged early in his *Journal*. Initially, it appears in a very famous passage coming in the midst of the four year period of despair. Fox had just finished with the fifth pastor, one Macham, and all had failed him in spiritual direction. Early in 1646, Fox was on his way to Coventry thinking about how all Christians, both Protestants and Catholics, are believers. Fox then declared that "the Lord opened to me that, if all were believers, then they were all born of God and passed from death to life, and that none were true believers but such; and though others said they were believers, yet they were not."[13]

The language of "opening" is the language of revelation. Two things are of significance here. First, the nature of the true believer was revealed to Fox. Secondly, true believers are believers because they are "born of God," one aspect of that birth being a passage from death to life. It is not difficult to understand the relationship of birth (or spiritual re-birth) and life. It does seem, however, that in Fox's world, as well as the contemporary, what is an experiential event frequently becomes a doctrinal article. Unfortunately, to be a believer becomes a matter of cognitive assent rather than a passage from death to life. In fact, the passage out of the condition of death requires an experience of conversion, a turning away from death and a turning toward the One who gives life. This is why Fox can "know" revelationally that some are not "true" believers—to be a believer is not a matter of what one says but what one experiences! In addition to being shown what the nature of a true believer was, Fox also was shown the true nature of a minister. The process of coming to be a believer is continued by the process which brings one into ministry. Fox recognized the call to discipleship entailed a call into ministry, not only turning one to God the redeemer, but leading one through ministry into the world.

So, Fox was able, as he walked along on a later Sunday morning, to say something about the nature of true ministers. He tells us that:

> ...the Lord opened unto me that being bred at Oxford or Cambridge was not enough to fit and qualify men to be ministers of Christ; and I stranged at it because it was the common belief of people. But I saw clearly, as the Lord opened it to me, and was satisfied, and admired the goodness of the Lord who had opened this thing unto me that morning, which struck at Priest Stephen's ministry, namely, that to be bred at Oxford or Cambridge was not enough to make a man fit to be a minister of Christ. So that which opened in me, I saw, struck at the priest's ministry.[14]

A number of significant issues emerge from this pregnant passage. First, Fox's language of "man" here referring to ministry could be misleading. Contrary to other institutional forms of religion in his time, Fox was, from the outset, quite clear that women not only have a right, but also a responsibility for ministry. This will be explored more fully in subsequent chapters.

Another issue is the recognition, which Quakers typically miss, that Fox was *not against* Oxford or Cambridge. What he declared was that being bred or educated there was not "enough" to "fit and qualify" persons for the ministry. Significantly, Fox does not say that going to *Oxbridge* is wrong. What he does, in a careful, Quaker sense, is to guard against any notion that education, particularly from a good or right place, is what makes a minister. To the contrary, as Fox and his Quaker successors argue, it is experience of God and the gift of the Holy Spirit which makes persons "fit and qualified" for ministry. Hence, Fox once more leads squarely back to the primacy of experience and the necessity of being "opened" to the Christ within who will be our teacher and guide.

The "opening" about the nature of the true believer and the true minister was an experience of revelation. This experience not only elicited particular feelings, but eventually provoked its own theological content. To have a good understanding of what revelation is helps one grasp what a powerful experience lies behind and is pointed at in the language of "opening." Langdon Gilkey offers an incisive look at what revelation means.

> Revelation, then, means the self-manifestation of the divine power and meaning on which all depends and in and through which all is fulfilled, that is to say, in our tradition, "God." At its most fundamental level, therefore, revelation means the communication of the divine *power* (being, life, health, and eternal life) of the divine *truth* (order, illumination, insight, and meaning), and of the divine *love* (mercy, forgiveness, and renewing, reuniting love).[15]

Although revelation is typically seen as a "theological" word, when one unpacks the content of this passage, one can understand the spirituality of which theology is a part.

Indeed, Fox's langauge of "opening" communicates the experiential nature of spirituality along with cognitive content. Gilkey's term, revelation, talks about it as communication of divine *power* and *love*. Truly, Fox was moved by his opening, and also was taken into a relationship of love by God and, then, for others. In addition to power and love, Fox was brought into a new understanding with insight, *truth*. This in itself was moving—something more than doctrinal assent. Gilkey adds, revelation "is a communication both of a new way of existing and a new way of understanding or of believing."[16]

This opening to the power, truth, and love of God did transform Fox and, consequently, bring him into a new way of relating to the world. The openings he experienced were the way he was led through the ocean of darkness into the ocean of light, from death to love. They were the experiential pathways from deadness to life. In Fox's case, there was not just *one* big opening, but a series through which he was converted. In this sense, his transformation was a process, rather than an event. What Fox realized about the nature of the true believer was what he began to realize about himself. In the same year as the first opening, Fox wrote:

At another time it was opened in me that God, who made the world, did not dwell in temples made with hands. This, at first, seemed a strange word because both priests and people used to call their temples or churches, dreadful places, and holy ground, and the temples of God. But the Lord showed me, so that I did see clearly, that he did not dwell in these temples which men had commanded and set up, but in people's hearts...[17]

Fox finished this passage with an allusion to Paul's word from II Corinthians 3:16-18 beginning with Paul's question, "Do you not know that you are God's temple and that God's Spirit dwells in you?" In fact, one can guess that through God's openings Fox discovered that he was a temple!

This was so powerful for Fox because now he was experientially realizing that he was a stranger to all; that God was dealing directly and immediately with him. God's presence and grace were not being mediated through a priest or by ecclesiastical sacraments. Thus begins the formation in Fox's spiritual life of a couple of keys to Quaker spirituality. First, is the ability of each and every human to experience God directly and without mediation from any other human or any institution. If there is that of God in every person, then God will speak to that in each person. The second characteristic of Quaker spirituality is the view of the church (ecclesiology) which develops as a result of experiencing God. In essence, the church, or meeting, is the place and occasion where people gather to experience individually and, then, corporately the presence of God. Rather than "take" sacraments, Quakers are "gathered" and become God's sacrament. The key to both aspects of Quaker spirituality is knowing God in one's *heart*.

Coming to discover that God can speak to one's condition presupposes one knows that condition. This usually requires an "opening" through which one sees and into which one can be led. (In a way, to come to know one has a heart.) This transforming process has sometimes been compared to realizing and accepting one's "nakedness." Rosemary Haughton writes:

To be naked does not mean simply to be unclothed, it means to remove (or to have stripped off) the normal defences and disguises of common life, by which sinful people protect themselves from too much knowledge of themselves or others. It means to be defenseless, intensely vulnerable.[18]

This appropriately describes Fox's stripping off process because he was left to struggle and to cope with turmoil. The openings did not automatically "fix" things. Fox told the reader:

> Now though I had great openings, yet great trouble and temptation came many times upon me, so that when it was day I wished for night, and when it was night I wished for day, and by reason of the openings I had in my troubles, I could say as David said, 'Day unto day uttereth speech, and night unto night showeth knowledge.' And when I had openings, they answered one another and answered the Scriptures, for I had great openings of the Scriptures...[19]

Fox apparently had a number of openings because here he consistently used the plural. Furthermore, these openings "answer." This is the language Fox used to describe how God through Christ "talks" to humans, addressing their hearts.

The first observation is a simple but profound one. That Fox talked about openings in the plural meant he had many; indeed, a number of them will be considered. There was not just one event, one opening, which was crucial. In fact, openings were the way into the process of experiencing God, developing the relationship and living the love. The Quaker doctrine of continuing revelation has this idea of multiple openings at its core. And to recall Gilkey's words on revelation, continuing revelation would be the fresh and refreshing communication of divine power, truth and love.

To see this fresh communication as a series of openings is a perceptive way to understand revelation as "continuing." Typically, in the debate about continuing revelation, the debate is not about a "process." And yet, for Quaker spirituality, that is key. Revelation, or openings, *continue* for persons involved in relationship with God.

Normally, the debate about continuing revelation focuses solely on *content*, whether through revelation God shows or discloses "more" truth or knowledge than the Bible contains. Here a fundamentalist position quite clearly answers negatively. Fundamentalists see the Bible as the source of all truth and knowledge; it is not a matter of interpretation. Quaker spirituality, along with many others, is not fundamentalist, which means all knowledge and truth about God is interpretative, whether indirectly from the Bible or directly through an opening by experience.

The Quaker understanding of revelation as "opening" underscores another key aspect of spirituality, namely, the emphasis upon experience. Insofar as one *continues* powerfully to experience God and has the experience of God *opening* one to truth and bringing one to love, one is experiencing *continuing revelation.* Power, truth and love, as Fox and Quakers describe it, may be an insight into Biblical truth already visible, but not "seen." In this image, continuing revelation functions either like the healing of a blind person who now can see what always was there, or as truth and knowledge which actually may be "new"—new in the sense that it goes beyond what actually is said in the Biblical witness, or have to do with an area not explicitly addressed in the Biblical text.

The Quaker way of speaking about God's ongoing work of opening (revealing) humans and the whole of creation to the divine plan of salvation is a creative way of talking about what the Roman Catholic and Orthodox communions mean by "tradition." Continuing revelation, tradition (even what Jews mean by halakhah, the rule to go by and haggadah, preaching/teaching) are all attempts to use the central Biblical witness to interpret how God continues to work in human hearts in history. They are attempts to say Biblical truth must be applied and interpreted in every new day, continually in fresh but authentic ways. Georges Florovsky, an Orthodox church historian, artfully describes what one can take to be at the core of Fox's understanding of God's openings to him personally and, later, to gathered groups of believers.

> The sacred history of redemption is still going on. It is now the history of the Church that is the body of Christ. The Spirit-Comforter is already abiding in the Church. No complete system of Christian faith is yet possible, for the Church is still on her pilgrimage. And the Bible is kept by the Church as a book of history to remind believers of the dynamic nature of the divine...[20]

Continuing revelation, then, is the ongoing dynamic engagement of God with humans in history. In this sense, continuing revelation is always the beginning of Quaker spirituality.

Indeed, Douglas Steere, who edited *Quaker Spirituality* in the Paulist Press series of the Classics of Western Spirituality, begins the story of Quaker spirituality with an account of continuing revelation. Steere was a visitor at the 1963 second session of the Vatican Council II when Cardinals Suenens (Belgium) and Ruffini (Sicily) debated this issue. Suenens effectively was speaking for the ongoing action of God's Spirit beyond the church's *magisterium*, the church's teaching. Steere remarked that:

> Happily, in my judgment at least, the commission accepted the suggestion of Cardinal Suenens. But Cardinal Ruffini with his usual clarity had raised a most searching question. Is the Apostolic Age really over? Does the Holy Spirit still speak to ordinary people? Is the guidance of the Holy Spirit still operative? Is all revelation concluded? It is at this point that an account of Quaker spirituality and its presuppositions might comfortably begin.[21]

As a major shaper of Quaker spirituality, Fox did not believe the movement of the Spirit had ceased nor had God desisted from speaking to ordinary women and men. No one told Fox this; he knew it because God through Christ Jesus "spoke to his condition."

This, then, brings one back to the second aspect of openings, namely, as Fox said, they "answered one another and answered the Scriptures."[22] When Fox declared his openings answered each other, he meant they became the means to interpret truth and knowledge as they were opened or disclosed to him. Answering each other further meant the openings maintained a consistency and coherency of *content* in what was being disclosed. Finally, to suggest the openings answered scripture meant the content of the disclosures was consistent with the material revealed in the Biblical witness. Certainly, when one talks about the development of Quaker doctrine (theology) or practice (ethics), it is important to note that continuing revelation acknowledges God does not reveal new or additional truths which are inconsistent with the spirit of the biblical witness as disclosed in the life and teaching of Jesus Christ, the Word incarnate.

Inasmuch as the primary focus for Fox in his openings was not doctrine but experience, it becomes clear why Fox saw and Quakers articulate, it is the current, ongoing work of the Holy Spirit which begins an account of Quaker spirituality. Fox knew the scriptures but it was only through the Spirit's opening to him that the scriptures began to speak as the living Christ addressed his condition. Without the Spirit, scripture becomes mere letters, breathless words.

Following the quotation where Fox excitedly described Christ Jesus speaking to his condition, he continued:

> My desires after the Lord grew stronger, and zeal in the pure knowledge of God and of Christ alone, without the help of any man, book, or writing. For though I read the Scriptures that spoke of Christ and of God, yet I knew him not but by revelation, as he who hath the key did open, and as the Father of life drew me to his Son by his spirit. And then the Lord did gently lead me along, and did let me see his love, which was endless and eternal, and surpasseth all the knowledge that men have in the natural state, or can get by history or books; and that love let me see myself as I was without him. And I was afraid of all company, for I saw them perfectly where they were, through the love of God which let me see myself. I had not fellowship with any people, priests, or professors, nor any sort of separated people, but with Christ, who hath the key and opened the door of light and life unto me.[23]

This passage is a rich vein for understanding the spiritual function of "opening." An opening is the door to power, love and truth, the pathway out of the ocean of darkness and death. As Fox said, Christ had the key and opened the door of light and life.

It is important to recognize that Christ has the key. In this sense one does well to recall that Fox was unable by his own efforts to escape from that ocean of darkness. As he said, he was "in the deep, under all, shut up." The door was closed and locked. It was not that he was passive; he was unable to open the door. It was Christ Jesus who opened it for him. With that opening, Fox was given the possibility for which his activity was designed.

One can understand and appreciate the formation of spirituality from the "movement" introduced by an opening. As Fox said, now God "drew" him to the Son of God, and furthermore, the Lord "did gently lead me along." Being led along enabled Fox to "see" the love of God, and, in that love, Fox was able to "see" his condition separate from God—the condition to which Christ Jesus spoke. What a powerful passage!

The movement afforded by an opening is noteworthy. God's act of drawing and leading is a gentle act. It is an act of *tenderness* — a term Fox used frequently. Quaker spirituality is not a violent, rough, abusive spirituality because the God who is experienced is gentle, tender and loving. Revelation shows this tenderness and experience knows it.

In a passage from 1647 at the end of his period of despair Fox writes:

> ...one day when I had been walking solitarily abroad and was come home, I was taken up in the love of God, so that I could not but admire the greatness of his love. And while I was in that condition it was opened unto me by the eternal Light and power, and I therein saw clearly that all was done and to be done in and by Christ, and how he conquers and destroys this tempter, the Devil and all his works, and is atop of him, and that all these troubles were good for me, and the temptations for the trial of my faith which Christ had given me. And the Lord opened me that I saw through all these troubles and temptations. My living faith was raised, that I saw all was done by Christ, the life, and my belief was in him. And when at any time my condition was veiled, my secret belief was stayed firm, and hope underneath held me, as an anchor in the bottom of the sea, and anchored my immortal soul to its Bishop, causing it to swim above the sea, the world where all the raging waves, foul weather, tempests, and temptations are. But oh, then did I see my troubles, trials, and temptations more than ever I had done! As the Light appeared, all appeared that is out of the Light, darkness, death, temptations, the unrighteous, the ungodly; all was manifest and see in the Light.[24]

At the outset one can see from this quotation basis for the *affective* character of Quaker spirituality. The language of love used by Fox described his experience of the God whose opening brought Fox into relationship.

In *A History of Christian Spirituality*, Urban Holms says that "radical Protestant spirituality is affective."[25] He puts Fox in this camp. As seen earlier, affective spirituality is characterized by an emphasis on the heart or emotions and clearly guided Fox's encounter with God's love. Fox saw, when he moved into the opening God provided, that love was endless, eternal and beyond knowledge. It was *love* more than knowledge which "touched" Fox and spoke to his condition. His condition was one of being separate from God; in love he felt embraced and loved for who he was. In this love he discovered a light by which he could see and a life into which he was drawn. He walked through the opening a new man.

That Fox emerged a new man is attested to in his own words. The beginning quotation of the second chapter states that Fox was "very much altered in countenance and person as if my body had been new moulded or changed."[26] This occurred in 1647 at the end of his period of despair. Fox continued by saying he was brought through the ocean of darkness and death by the power of Christ and concluded the paragraph in this way.

> Even through that darkness I was brought, which covered-over all the world, and which chained down all, and shut up all in the death. And the same eternal power of God, which brought me through these things, was that which afterwards shook the nations, priests, professors, and people. Then could I say I had been in spiritual Babylon, Sodom, Egypt, and the grave; but by the eternal power of God I was come out of it, and was brought over it and the power of it, into the power of Christ. And I saw the harvest white, and the Seed of God lying thick in the ground, as ever did what that was sown outwardly, and none to gather it; and for this I mourned with tears.[27]

Fox was eloquent in this passage about the *power* of God through Christ which delivered him through the openings. Gilkey's words on revelation states that revelation communicates divine truth, love and power. Clearly, in his openings, Fox experienced all three.

There remains much which could be said about openings, but as the last quotation indicates, an opening ultimately leads one into ministry. In this movement, Fox's burden shifted from his own person to a burden for the world. Now, knowing there is "a way out" of darkness and death, he received the burden to open others out of their darkness and death. For Fox, the love of God was central to his experience of Christ having the key which opened the door of light and life.

To say that the love of God is central for Fox's understanding of God's work in the world is both unoriginal and yet profoundly significant. Obviously Fox was not the first Christian thinker to suggest the centrality of God's love. Indeed in some way, anyone standing in the Christian tradition stands on the scriptural dictum that

"God so loved the world that he gave his only Son, that whoever believes in him should not perish but have eternal life." (John 3:16) One could even push this passage as an organizing principle for Fox's spirituality. To perish is the fate of those whose condition is the ocean of darkness and death. Eternal life is the gift of a new condition, one where God's love touches and leads into relationship. In seeing this *love in action*, one understands the essence of Fox's spirituality. Love is central as the operative principle which shows (reveals) human nature (sin) and lets one *see* where God is leading.

Learning to love required a kind of renunciation. One must, Alan Jones challenges, "renounce the other for the sake of the other."[28] In God's action through Jesus Christ it can be attested that God has given up self for the other, *pro nobis* (for us). Rosemary Haughton used the language of "breakthrough" to describe this passionate exchange on behalf of humans.

> ...the nature of God is love, and the origin of love, the Father from whom is life, pours himself out in total giving in the Beloved, who, in his human nature, receives the outpouring of love, and receives it *as human*, that is, as coinherent in all human life and in all creation. Therefore (since sin is the condition in which created life is) he receives it in a condition which "blocks" the flow of love *in* return. It is the work of incarnate Wisdom to make that longed-for return possible.
>
> The cry of Jesus on the cross at the very end was, therefore, the cry of awareness that all was indeed accomplished, brought to its consumation. He knew that he could, at last, give back to the One he loved the unshackled fullness of love, and in so doing *carry with him* on the surge of that passion the love which is the essential being of all creation. That is, in a sense, the movement of resurrection, or rather it is the moment at which the process begins, for the resurrection is not a single event but the ever—extending 'outflow' of the energy previously damned up by the power of sin and death.[29]

This extended passage from Haughton gives in contemporary language something of the feeling which characterized Fox's breakthrough. It demonstrates why love is central and Jesus Christ is key.

Love is the key for Fox in the first place because of its revelatory function. It has already been pointed out the nature of revelation as "opening." Love functions in this context because it is that which enables us to see ourselves *as* we are and *for what* we are. In the midst of a longer passage cited earlier, Fox says this about love:

> And then the Lord did gently lead me along, and did let me see his love, which was endless and eternal, and surpasseth all the knowledge that men have in the natural state...and that love let me see myself as I was without him.[30]

Fox continued by realizing he had been in the deep, all shut up. Love, then, is the medium of God's leading. God "gently" led Fox to open his eyes and discover God's care. In this amazing opening, Fox realized that he was not alone—God loved him. Furthermore, Fox recognized he was not stuck or shut up, but through God's love he was free.

Interestingly, Fox used the language of "seeing" God's love. This language communicated something of the recognition of the experience of revelation—namely, he came *to know* both his own condition and the love of God which released him from the ocean of darkness and death. Seeing also communicates something about the *experience itself.* To see God's love is to feel it, to be embraced by it and taken up in it. It is more than intellectual assurance; it is emotional envelopment and spiritual formation. In that love Fox was home. Once more, he states, "one day when I had been walking solitarily abroad and was come home, I was taken up in the love of God, so that I could not but admire the greatness of his love."[31] Indeed, Fox may have physically found his way home, but in God's love he discovered the true, eternal home!

The home of God's love is being found in a place where one belongs, where one is accepted for who one is and allowed and nurtured to "grow up" into whom one can become. In a paradoxical way, Christian disciples set out on journeys which might carry them physically significant distances from their earthly home. And yet, disciples are always "at home" in God's love. In the midst of movement, they know security and serenity. Fox had come to see this and to know it. Into this love Fox was taken and in it he experienced the joy of a heart which had fallen in love!

The revelatory language of love as Gilkey used it, states that love communicated by God's action means mercy, forgiveness, renewing and reuniting. This love from God brings one into relationship. With God's love one is, as it were, re-made or re-created. It is work (*re-*

58

making), but it will finally be fun (*recreation*). Alan Jones gives a clue about this joyous journeying into the love of God. Paradoxically, the beginning of that journey brings one to the abyss, the place of despair.

> It is there, and only there, that love worthy of the name is born. It is only at the edge of the abyss that the parody that passes for love is unmasked. Power plays, manipulation, and unhealthy dependence often masquerade as love. Love that is energized by anxiety and insecurity is hardly love at all. For some of us, it's the best that we can do. The only thing that releases us from the bondage of our anxiety - dominated false loves is the experience (however faint and short-lived) of unsolicited, unconditional, disinterested love...As a believer, I am slowly coming to realize that God loves us like that. He delights in us. He enjoys us. When such a truth begins to take hold of a believer, the world is changed.[32]

Fox's world did change through the love of God as Christ Jesus began to speak to his condition. The love of God, as Fox experienced it, was both transforming and vitalizing. By the love of God he was delivered from death and brought into life. In his own words from 1647 he declared that:

> ...I saw the great love of God, and I was filled with admiration at the infiniteness of it; and then I saw what was cast out from God, and what entered into God's kingdom, and how by Jesus, the opener of the door by his heavenly key, the entrance was given. And I saw death, how it had passed upon all men and oppressed the Seed of God in man and in me, and how I in the Seed came forth, and what the promise was to.[33]

In fact, through this love of God, Fox was delivered from death into God's kingdom. And the key means by which love delivered him into the kingdom was Christ Jesus.

In this sense, the chapter rightfully ends as it began—with the christological note—recognizing that Jesus Christ is the key to the love of God, the doorway into the kingdom. To find that door is to be given light in order to see where one is in darkness and to see how and where one is being led out of the darkness into the light of God's presence and the freedom of God's grace. In this sense, Jesus Christ does open up one's condition. Jesus Christ does turn one from the false self, idols and illusion to the true God and to God's kingdom. In this opening and turning, one is brought into the knowledge of the Spirit's working, making disciples and ministers of the loving God. When this happens, one's response will be that of Fox, "my heart did leap for joy."

60

IV

THE OCEAN OF LIGHT

And the Lord answered that it was needful I should have a
sense of all conditions, how else should I speak to all
conditions; and in this I saw the infinite love of God. I saw
also that there was an ocean of darkness and death, but an
infinite ocean of light and love, which flowed over the ocean
of darkness. And in that also I saw the infinite love of God;
and I had great openings.[1]

This opening quotation is the same one used in the initial chapter
which developed Fox's understanding of the ocean of darkness.
Here, however, the focus is on the ocean of light. Darkness and light
balance nicely, but in Fox's metaphorical way of describing human
conditions as oceans, he balances death with love! To maintain
symmetry in the metaphor, one might have expected "life" rather than
"love" to counterbalance "death."

That Fox uses "love" to balance "death" is not surprising when one
takes seriously the christological key to his experience of God. God
through the Lord Jesus spoke to Fox and answered his need. Through
the love of God, Fox was brought out of darkness into the light and
passed through death into life. One has to live to love—or
conversely, if one loves and is loved, one is alive! And the nature of
divine love is infinite, which means to be loved infinitely by God is

to be given eternal life.

In classical Christian language, Fox had a saving experience of Jesus Christ. In traditional Quaker language, Fox was brought into the divine light, which light he came to know and understand as Christ Jesus. This chapter briefly details the process of coming to live in that light. To live in that light is nothing other than being in the ocean of light and love.

Again, in the opening quotation Fox declared that he *saw* the infinite love of God. One might well ask, *how does one see* infinite love? At the end of the quotation Fox gave a hint when he said he had great openings. Obviously, Fox used the language of "seeing" in a metaphorical sense. He "sees" in the sense of understands. What he understood was given to him revelationally, through an opening. But, care must be taken not merely to intellectualize what a profound experience it was for Fox. The language of "flowing" describes how the ocean of light overcomes darkness in affective, dynamic terms. When Fox said the ocean of light and love *flows* over the other ocean, he suggested an experience of movement, of consequence and of victory. Darkness had been overcome and death had been defeated. The Prologue to John's gospel states similarly that "the light shines in the darkness, and the darkness has not overcome it." (John 1:5)

The spiritual language of "flowing" was experientially effective for Fox because of the implied movement . To see the love of God, in the sense of being involved, was to come to be in that ocean of light and love and to flow over the ocean of darkness. By his own efforts Fox was able only to drown in that darkness. However, through the loving act of God, he was caught up and moved out of that darkness. Using contemporary language, Fox was able to "go with the flow!"

Fox gives a fairly clear idea how the flow of God's love comes, picks one up and moves into that light which is God's loving presence. In this passage Fox no longer had himself in mind, but spoke out of his ministry. Nevertheless, the process is basically the same for all humans as they become buoyed by the ocean of love.

> As I was walking I heard old people and work people to say,
> 'He is such a man as never was, he knows people's thoughts,'
> for I turned them to the divine light of Christ and his spirit
> that let them see all their thoughts, words, and actions, that
> were evil, that they had thought or spoken, or acted; with
> which light they might see their sins and with the same light
> they might see their saviour, Christ Jesus, to save them from

their sins, and that there was their first step to peace—to stand still in the light that showed their sin and transgressions and showed them how they were strangers to the covenant of promise, without God in the world, and in the Fall of old Adam, and in the darkness and death; and with the same light they may see Christ that died for them, who is their way to God and their redeemer and saviour.[2]

The process Fox described commences by *turning* people to the light of Christ. Having turned, people are able to *see*. Finally, with the light to see, people are *shown* things. This, then, is the process by which people are brought from the ocean of darkness into the ocean of light.

The last chapter indicated the process of conversion begins with a turning, *metanoia*, which was related most with an "opening." In this present context, Fox used the more traditional language of "turning," and even described his own instrumental role in the process. He narrated how he "turns" people to the divine light. This language and its impact appears copiously throughout the *Journal* and in Quaker literature as a whole. In some cases, Fox talked about turning people to the light of Christ and, in other instances, Fox simply noted the power of Christ himself turned people. A powerful example of this turning is seen when Fox journeyed to Romney and shared ministry among the Baptists (1655). Fox declared that:

> ...many were shaken with the power of God, and the life sprang up in them...And a great convincement there was that day, and many were turned from the darkness to the divine light of Christ...[3]

Once again, turning is the initial movement from one ocean to another.

Fox explicitly said one turns from the darkness to the divine light of Christ. In the process of turning to the light, people become able to "see" their "thoughts, words, and actions, that were evil." In a word, Fox declared the initial effect of turning to the light of Christ was to see one's sins. In the darkness, one's sins were hidden from one's eyes, and were committed through will and habits to thoughts, words and actions which were destructive to oneself and negative in one's world.

Amazingly, one of the predictable experiential components of this turning is the feeling of disruption. Time and time again, Fox talked about the "shaking" which marked the turning out of darkness to the light of Christ. The quotation just cited speaks of many being "shaken with the power of God." In Fox's spirituality, shaking is the phenomenological result of the experience of God's power, a result of the transcendent breaking into one's life. It is "disruptive" insofar as it breaks through the routines and habits of the old self, and is really the initial step of spiritual formation. Fox's description is not novel and can be better understood by looking at Robert Mulholland's *Shaped by the Word.* He says:

> The first aspect of spiritual formation is what I call "breaking the crust."...The core of spiritual formation is the process of breaking the crust of self and bringing forth a new creation in the image of Christ — breaking the garbled, debased, distorted word we have become, and bringing forth the word God speaks us forth to be in the world.[4]

Mulholland's description of breaking the crust of the self is a good way to understand Fox's experience of how people's hearts are shaken by the inbreaking of God's power.

Early in Fox's ministry after his period of despair (1648) he had a vision of this inbreaking power of God which turned people to the light of Christ. Fox said:

> ...as I was sitting in a Friend's house in Nottinghamshire...I saw there was a great crack to go throughout the earth, and a great smoke to go as the crack went; and that after the crack there should be a great shaking. This was the earth in people's hearts, which was to be shaken before the Seed of God was raised out of the earth. And it was so; for the Lord's power began to shake them...[5]

Clearly, then, the Lord's power shakes and cracks the crustiness of human hearts and opens one up to be able to turn to the light of Christ. Two aspects of Fox's spirituality emerge at this point. People feel themselves being opened up and turning and, secondly, they realize their ability to begin seeing from where they came (darkness and sin) and where they are going (light and wholeness). In Fox's imagery, the earth of the people's hearts was evil thoughts, words and actions, which must be broken up and turned from. Not only do they see the negative side of where they have been, but they also *focus* on where they are being drawn. Fox eloquently put it, "with the same light they might see their saviour, Christ Jesus, to save them from their sins, and that there was their first step to peace."[6] The initial result of their turning opens them up to new possibilities and a new place, the beginning of the birth of the new self.

This seeing is itself *transitional.* As people are brought into the dawn of the light of Christ, they are able to see what God shows. Being led into that place of light, they discover that they have come to stand in that place. Indeed, Fox suggested in this new place they will be shown fully who they were and whom they are becoming.

With this showing they are brought to a place of rest, a place of salvation and potential wholeness. This culminates the process of turning; the seeker has found the object of the search. It does not mean the journey is over and the destination has been reached; rather, the real spiritual journey can now begin.

Indeed, people are shown in the place of light not only something of their old selves in the place of darkness and death, but they are able to see with anticipation into the future to which they are being called and formed. As Mulholland states, it is to become the "word God speaks us forth to be in the world." In Fox's language, the power of God which shook them out of sin will anchor them in a relationship of the covenant of promise. Through the salvific death of Christ, a "way" into light and life not only had opened up but reached out to bring them into this way. Even though already alive, they are reborn, made new.

This discovery of a way enlightened by the light of Christ is more than theological acrobatics. Fox truly had an experience of being made new, of discovering he had been given a new self, and had been restored to the state or condition of Adam, and even, more. Through the Spirit, Fox had been given the vision to see paradise and, more powerfully, to live in the paradisaical condition. In what must be one of the more eloquently metaphorical passages in his *Journal,* Fox described his newness and the creation renewed.

> Now I was come up in the spirit through the flaming sword into the paradise of God. All things were new, and all the creation gave another smell unto me than before, beyond what words can utter. I knew nothing but pureness, and innocency, and righteousness, being renewed up into the image of God by Christ Jesus, so that I say I was come up to

the state of Adam which he was in before he fell. The creation was opened to me, and it was showed me how all things had their names given them according to their nature and virtue...But I was immediately taken up in spirit, to see into another or more steadfast state than Adam's innocency, even into a state in Christ Jesus, that should never fall. And the Lord showed me that such as were faithful to him in the power and light of Christ, should come up into that state in which Adam was before he fell, and which the admirable works of the creation and the virtues thereof, may be known, through the openings of that divine Word of wisdom and power by which they were made. Great things did the Lord lead me into, and wonderful depths were opened unto me, beyond what can by words be declared; but as people come into subjection to the spirit of God, and grow up in the image and power of the Almighty, they may receive the Word of wisdom, that opens all things, and come to know the hidden unity in the Eternal Being.[7]

This description of what the ocean of light looks like and feels like leaves one tempted merely to conclude by saying, "Amen."

Yet, a number of themes from this passage give further shape to Fox's spirituality. Perhaps the first thing observed is the language of directionality. In the Spirit, Fox was "come up." This language of movement *upward* is the opposite of the downward direction and the sense of entrapment which described the ocean of darkness. There, one recalls, Fox talked about being "in the deep, under all, shut up." In the Spirit, Fox was not only opened up but brought up—by implication and in fact—up out of the darkness of the deep death into the light of full life. He came through the flaming sword into the paradise of God.

Coming up out of darkness by the Spirit into paradise, Fox knew he had to pass through the flaming sword. This clearly is drawn from the biblical imagery of Genesis 3 which tells of the fall of Adam. In effect, Fox used the fall as a foil to narrate the story of what might be called "the Rise." God's work of salvation is the work of *restoring* and *renewing*. After sinning, Adam and Eve received the judgment of God; they received garments to cover their nakedness and were expelled from the garden.

Then the Lord God said, "Behold, the man has become like

one of us, knowing good and evil; and now, lest he put forth
his hand and take also of the tree of life, and eat, and live for
ever"—therefore the Lord God sent him forth from the
garden of Eden, to till the ground from which he was taken.
He drove out the man; and at the east of the garden of Eden
he placed the cherubim, and a flaming sword which turned
every way, to guard the way to the tree of life. (Gen. 3:22-
24)

It is important to understand the fall of Adam and Eve and their
expulsion in order to understand the breathtaking nature of Fox's experience and the challenge and profundity of his spirituality. Through
God's work in the Spirit, Fox emerged in a state higher and better than
Adam's original, pre-fallen state. Fox and, by implication all who
come to know God, will be led back up into paradise itself! Quaker
spirituality attests to the graceful restoration of humans to Eden. Or,
as Jesus would prayerfully put it, "thy kingdom come. Thy will be
done, on earth as it is in heaven." (Matthew 6:10) Indeed, what Fox
experienced was an inauguration into this kingdom and a teaching
about kingdom living.

God's kingdom is discovered in the newness of the old creation;
it is seen by turning to the light which illumines the darkness of the
old creation. Fox provocatively declared that all creation gave
another smell. This was not simply the incense of the altar, but it was
the creative fragrance of the world experienced as a garden. In this
garden, Fox experienced the original purity of the relationship with
God and humanity (Adam and Eve). As Fox said, "I knew nothing
but pureness, and innocency, and righteousness." These clearly are
descriptive terms of one justified by grace, restored to communion
with God and having come into the light. That Fox had creation in
mind even as he talked about re-creation is apparent when he further
acknowledged he was "being renewed up into the image of God by
Christ Jesus."

Once again, Fox used the spiritual language of verticality. He was
"renewed up," which suggests to be brought into the light is to be
brought "up." Indeed, experientially one feels "lighter." Not without
reason is the classical language of the "burden" of one's sins
employed. To lose the image of God is to fall away or down; renewal
is to be brought back up. Indeed, Fox does not lose the image;
rather, it merely is defaced and debased in sin and the darkness which
is sin. Renewal is the exposure of darkness and the eradication of

sin.

In fact, Fox was restored to the pre-fall state of Adam and Eve. But this was not the end; indeed, Fox continued to say he was taken up in the Spirit to see a state more permanent than was possible for Adam and Eve, namely, that state or condition of Christ Jesus which precludes even the possibility of falling away into sin and darkness. In spiritually revolutionary terms, the Lord "showed" Fox that all who were faithful to the power and light of Christ should come into that state and, by implication, live in and from that condition. This, of course, is the experiential and theological source of the Quaker doctrine of *perfection.*

That Quaker spirituality has as one of its hallmarks a perspective that humans can not only talk about but live "perfectly," has always been provocative. It is provocative because it seems haughty to suggest as a possibility and has led many ecclesiastical persons to denounce it as outright theological guffoonery. Early in Fox's *Journal,* one sees how this riled his critics. In 1647, he talked about moving from Lancashire to Manchester where some "professors" (one who makes a profession of faith) were convinced but others "were in a rage, all pleading for sin and imperfection, and could not endure to hear talk of perfection, and of an holy and sinless life."[8] Perfection has to do with coming under the influence of God's power and in that influence being empowered to live perfectly. In contrast to those who were convinced (turned) by the power of God's truth and were led to perfection, Fox stated a truth about those still in the condition of sin: "they were chained under darkness and sin, which they pleaded for, and quenched the tender thing in them."[9]

The key to perfection in Quaker spirituality is not to begin the discussion with a squabble over whether Fox literally meant "sinless." The key is once more christological—perfection for the believer hinges on the experience of Christ Jesus' saving and perfecting action in one's heart. Perfection, as both possibility and actuality, is rooted and grounded in the experience of God's love graciously bringing the one stuck in darkness to the light. Both in terms of initiation and sustenance, *grace* is the key.

Indeed, it is simple to show Fox began in the christological context of Christ Jesus through grace bringing the faithful up out of darkness into the light. During his ministry in Bristol in 1660 Fox wrote:

> ...all might come to receive Christ Jesus the substance by his
> light, spirit, grace, and faith, and live and walk in him the

redeemer and saviour. And all images and likenesses man has made, either of things in heaven or in earth to himself or for himself, hath been since he lost the image and likeness of God that God made him in. But now Christ was come to redeem, translate, convert, and regenerate man all out of all these things that he hath set up in the Fall, and out of the true types, figures, and shadows, and out of death and darkness, up into the light, and life, and image, and likeness of God again as man and woman were in before they fell.[10]

Through the transforming and restoring work of Christ, humans take on once more the image and likeness of their original creative condition. In the initial creation account in Genesis, God's creative words state, "Let us make man in our image, after our likeness...So God created man in his own image, in the image of God he created him; male and female he created them." (Gen. 2:26-27) Fox understood this image and likeness also included perfection. When this image and likeness are lost, imperfection characterizes the condition of darkness and death. The saving work of Christ Jesus is the re-creative work of restoring the image and likeness and, consequently, the possibility of perfection. Insofar as people actually experience this graceful transforming work in their hearts, they actualize the perfection of walking in the newness of life.

Fox continues to be both clear and provocatively steadfast on this point. Continuing the words at Bristol he stated:

And a great deal of work we had with the priests and professors pleading for imperfection. But I did let them see how Adam and Eve were perfect before they fell...how the imperfection came by the Fall, through man and woman's hearkening to the devil that was out of Truth...And Christ saith, 'Be ye perfect even as my heavenly father is perfect,' for he who was perfect comes to make man and woman perfect again and bring them again to the state God made them in; so he is the maker up of the breach and the peace betwixt God and man.[11]

The breathtaking character of Quaker perfection is its radicalness in belief to what the full transforming work of God can accomplish! Fox was unwilling to exercise "eschatological reserve," that is, to say one can be perfect, but not until heaven. No, the radical nature of

God's grace can, in Fox's estimation, bring one experientially into the intimacy of relationship with God which befits kingdom-living.

Fox minced no words when he talked about misleading promises made by other religious groups. He declared:

> ...all the sects in Christendom have pretended to build up Adam and Eve's fallen house and when they have got people's money they tell them the house cannot be perfected here; and so their house lies as it did.
>
> But I told them Christ was come freely, who hath perfected for ever by one offering all them that are sanctified, and renews them up in the image of God, as man and woman were in before they fell; and makes man and woman's house as perfect again as God had made them at the first.[12]

The idea of perfection has pointed to a significant feature in Quaker spirituality, and launches a discussion of the human experience of finding and living in the light of Christ. Although Fox did not often use the language of the kingdom, coming to the light of Christ within meant coming to the kingdom. Following almost immediately upon his Pendle Hill vision of 1652, Fox traveled to Lancaster. There on a Sunday morning he declared he had a "great meeting in the street of soldiers and people" and continued to say he:

> ...declared the word of life and the everlasting Truth to them, and showed them their teacher, Christ Jesus...and so turned them to the light of Christ, the heavenly man, and to the spirit of God in their own hearts and where they might find God and Christ and his kingdom and know him their teacher.[13]

In this passage Fox lumps together a number of concepts describing the human experience of discovering the light within.

In what could seem like an almost careless theological manner, Fox declared that humans discover in their own hearts their inward teacher, the light which is the Spirit of God and Christ's kingdom. Suffice it here to say the interest is not in Fox as a systematic theologian but rather with his developing spirituality; that is, how he talked about the underlying spiritual experience. In this sense, his words are both rich and suggestive.

The light of Christ had not only a theological, but also particularly a spiritual role to play in the life of George Fox. This concept of the light is especially related to an inward experience. Indeed, the *experience* is crucial and central for Fox and for Quaker spirituality. This comes through very clearly in an exchange between Fox and Henry Vane, (described by John Nickalls as a parliamentarian and mystic.)[14]

And I was moved of the Lord to speak to him of the true light which Christ doth enlighten every man that cometh into the world withal, and he saith, 'Believe in the light that ye may become children of the light'; and how that Christ had promised to his disciples to send them the Holy Ghost, the spirit of truth, which should lead them into all truth, which we witnessed, and how that the grace of God which brought salvation and appeared unto all men and was the saints' teacher in the apostles' days and so it was now.

Then, says he, 'None of this doth reach to my experience.' 'Nay,' said I, 'then how camest though in if thou didst not by believing in the light, as Christ commands? And how comest thou into truth if thou hast not been led by the spirit of truth which led the disciples into all truth, which Christ promised to send them? And how camest thou to know salvation if it be not by the grace of God which brings it, which taught the saints? And therefore what is thy experience of and in?"[15]

Fox clearly was speaking out of his own experience in this passage. Although he used the scriptural language drawn from John's gospel of the light (John 1:9), Fox's primary concern was to ask about Henry Vane's experience. Indeed, Henry Vane allowed he had no experiential knowing comparable to Fox's.

Fox then asked him, "how camest thou in?" This is the key concern for Fox; except by *experience* of the light, spirit and grace, how does one enter into relationship with God? To experience Christ's light is to feel drawn into relationship and to know the work of salvation. Indeed, Fox used the classical language of salvation to describe the divine-human relationship. Christ's work of salvation is the *drawing into* relationship, a *knowing* one's condition transformed by grace. This drawing and knowing is more than cognition or doctrine, it is a felt experience. *It happens!*

The only thing which happened to Henry Vane was he concluded

Fox was mad! Fox observed "so Friends that were with me stranged to see his darkness and impatience...and I did see he was vain, and high, and proud, and conceited..."[16] Not to be in the light is to be in the darkness. For Fox, coming to be in the light was a *felt* experience, an affective spirituality. In 1652 at a church in Dalton, Fox said he "declared the word of life to the people, turning them from darkness to light and from the power of Satan to God..."[17] One important note is the turning does not move from impotence to power, but rather from one power (of Satan) to another (of God). The ocean of darkness has its own power of destruction and death. The turning is a move away from that grip to a new power, a power unto life! In the light one can see; in this new power one can feel new life. Clearly for Fox this is the gospel, the good news.

The gospel, then, is something felt, a power, rather than simply a book to be read. In that same year, 1652, just before the visit to Dalton, Fox was at Aldingham in the same general area around Swarthmore Hall in what is now the Cumbria district. Fox wrote that on Sunday:

> ...I declared to the people the Gospel, the Truth, the light of Jesus Christ in their own hearts, which he had enlightened them that they might all come to, that let them see all that ever they had done, and said, and acted, and that would be their teacher when they were about their labours. The priest told me Matthew, Mark, Luke and John were the Gospel, I told him the Gospel was the power of God.[18]

For Fox, then, the good news was not the printed page but the light that shone in the hearts of people. This light acts upon one, draws one in, and empowers one to live in God's kingdom.

Rather than deal doctrinally with the concept of light, the spiritual, experiential effects of this engagement need to be pursued as an empowering agent unto life. In 1656 Fox wrote a letter to Friends concerning those who were "young and tender in the Truth." This pastoral letter spoke to the power felt while experiencing the light.

> For now you know the power of God, which is the Cross of Christ, and are come to it, which crucifies you from the state that Adam and Eve were in the Fall, and so from the world; by which power of God you come to see the state Adam and Eve were in before they fell...Yea, I say and to a state higher,

the Seed, Christ the second Adam, by whom all things were made...And the way is Christ the light, the life, the Truth, and the saviour, the redeemer, the sanctifier, the justifier; and so in his power and light and life who is the way to God, conversion, regeneration, and translation are known, from death to life, darkness to light, and from the power of Satan to God again.[19]

This amazing passage summarizes all that has been said thus far.

Upon examining the spiritual empowerment of the light of Christ, two aspects are discovered. The first aspect is related to the christological act of redemption. Initially, the power of God is the power of the cross. This is the power which converts and transforms one, leading one out of darkness to the light, and bringing one up out of the ocean of death to life. This power "crucifies" the old self of sin, and brings one into a condition or state even higher than Adam and Eve knew.

A second aspect of the power of the light is related to the ministry of the new creature. This in itself has a two-fold character. The first is the power from which one speaks the gospel word and out of which one lives the gospel witness. With frequency, Fox and early Friends spoke "in the power of God." For example, in 1651, Fox traveled to the church at Beverley and, as was usual, on Sunday when the preacher finished, Fox commenced!

And when he had done, I was moved to speak to him and the people in the mighty power of God, of the truth of God and the day of the Lord, and the Light of Christ within them, and of the spirit, and of God's teaching by the spirit, and that God that made the world did not dwell in the temples made with hands. The power of the Lord was so strong as it struck a mighty dread amongst the people.[20]

Feeling and speaking out of the power of the Lord was repeated many times. Focusing on ministry in chapter 6, it is important now to get an experiential sense of this power of the light of Christ.

The power of God is experienced as a dynamic, moving force. As the last quotation indicated, it has the ability to change the course of action for people. It causes emotional change as well as physical change in individuals. Fox employed a range of metaphorical ways of describing how people experienced this effective power. For instance, he used sensual language to symbolize the reality of God's presence. This feeling quality comes through vividly when Fox traveled to Cleveland in 1651 and noted "...there was a people that had tasted of the power of God."[21] Using the language of tasting suggests the eucharistic or communion motif. Although Fox and early Friends were to dispense with the outward elements of baptism and communion, they eagerly retained the sense that rebirth into God's Spirit through the power of the cross meant to be placed in communication with the *real presence* of God experienced as power.

This real presence of God is the place from which one speaks the gospel word and from which one lives the gospel witness. This speaking and loving can only be done from a place of strength, strength made possible by the power of God. Although speaking and living out of this gospel power appeared dangerous, it was a safe and secure place for Fox because to be in God's power is to be under God's protection.

When Fox spoke about God's protective power, he did so on two levels. The first was real, though simplistic, namely, God physically protects the loved ones. Particularly, this appeared to be the case in some examples of ministry. Upon returning to Johnstons (now Perth) Scotland from which he had been banished, Fox wrote that "the Lord's power came over them all and they had no power to touch me..."[22] From this encounter Fox passed back over the Firth of Forth to Edinburgh. Once more, he shared a glimpse into his feelings as he wrote "I bid Robert Widders follow me, and so in the dread and power of the Lord we came to the first two sentries; and the Lord's power came so over them that we passed by them without any examination."[23] Fox concluded this triumphal entry account by saying:

> So I saw and felt that I went over their very muskets, cannons, pistols, pikes, and very sword-ends. And the Lord's power and immediate hand carried us over the heads of them all.[24]

This kind of sentiment interpreted as God's protective hand is found in many places within the *Journal* and other Quaker writing. It can be labeled simplistic, not because it is naive or wrong, but because there obviously are different experiences, ones of suffering and tribulation which must also be seen in the larger context of God's power. So, even Fox concluded that God's protective power did not have as the only goal the physical or emotional sparing of God's loved ones.

Certainly Fox argued that God's concern and love for humans extended to their whole lives. But this power of God's concern finally must be seen in the ultimate, eternal context of the divinity. The protective safety of God's power ultimately means one lives rather than dies; one lives in the light rather than darkness. Fox assured those in the Spirit, but also in peril, that they would conquer because Christ already had prevailed. The security of this faith, buoyed by the hope of confidence and enveloped in the felt love of the Spirit, leads into the protective harbor of a relationship of trust and safety. Culminating this word about the protective power of God and moving to the next aspect of the experiential affect of coming into the light, Fox's pastoral advice was sound.

> You will hear and feel and see the power of God, as your faith is all in it, preaching when you do not hear words, to bind, to chain, to limit, to frustrate, that nothing shall rise nor shall come forth, but what is in the power. And with that you will let up, and open every spring, plant, and spark, in which will be your joy and refreshment.[25]

In a captivating fashion, Fox used the affective language of hearing, feeling, and seeing God's power. To feel that power which is the light's effect leads to a place of peace and joy; to live in the light is to live in the peaceable kingdom.

Earlier this chapter previewed how one's turning to the light brought one into a condition of peace.[26] There Fox identified the initial aspect of turning to Christ's light as salvation from sin, "their first step to peace." This implied there were additional "steps." Fox probably did not mean steps in a hierarchical, developmental manner, but a growing into the state or condition of peace and joy which befits one who stands and lives in the light. Fox articulated this ever-abiding presence of God's peace in an epistle to Friends written in 1657 as he rested at Swarthmore.

> All Friends of the Lord everywhere, whose minds are turned in towards the Lord, take heed and hearken to the light within you, which is the light of Christ and of God; which will call your minds within, as you love it, which is abroad in the creatures. So your minds may be renewed and by it turned to God with this which is pure, to worship the living

76

God...And the light of God, which calls the mind out of the
creatures, turns it to God, into a being of endless joy and
peace.[27]

The language of joy and peace is biblical, classical Christian language
for the kingdom. For Fox, this state of being characterized those
who lived in the light.
A final experiential aspect of coming to this light is the feeling of
being blessed. Not a great deal of attention has been paid to this idea
in many Christian circles, but it forms an important aspect of Quaker
spirituality. It is human nature to want to feel good! Being blessed
includes this good feeling but adds even more dimensions; as Paul
Tillich noted, being blessed characterizes "those who are grasped by
the divine Spirit."[28] Tillich continued:

The word designates a state of mind in which Spiritual
Presence produces a feeling of fulfillment which cannot be
disturbed by negativities in other dimensions. Neither bodily
nor psychological suffering can destroy the "transcendent
happiness" of being blessed. In finite beings this positive
experience is always united with the awareness of its
contrary, the state of unhappiness, despair, condemna-
tion.[29]

As Tillich described blessedness, it is a state which has both an
affective (feeling) dimension and a cognitive (thinking) dimension.
People experience fulfillment, the peace and joy, of being in relationship with a loving God. They also know cognitively about this state
because of their real deliverance from its opposite, the ocean of
darkness and death.
In language less academic and more affective than Tillich, Fox
wrote about blessings. In a letter to Oliver Cromwell in 1655, Fox was
spiritually eloquent when he said:

Live in the Lord's power and life, then to thee he will give
wisdom, and the pure feeling thou wilt come into, whereby
thy soul will be refreshed and it will be thy delight to do the
will of God, and thy meat and drink, as thou in the pure
eternal power, counsel, will, and wisdom of God dwellest...In
what thou dost for the Lord God thou shalt have peace and

the blessing... [30]

Fox encouraged Cromwell to live in the light, and find the place of pure feeling, the delight in the Lord and love of God. There, in a blessed condition, he would be refreshed from the toil of life and nurtured for living his spiritual life. The blessed state is not an occasion for passivity nor an invitation for inactivity. Rather, it is the occasion for learning and an invitation for doing. This unfolds upon examining the words of Fox who described a meeting at Edge Hill in Warwickshire in 1656. There in the midst of Ranters and other "rude people," Fox declared:

And the Lord's everlasting Truth and word of life reached over all and in all, that all was chained. And many that day were turned to the Lord Jesus Christ by his power and spirit, and came to sit under his blessed, everlasting, free teaching and feeding with his eternal and heavenly food.[31]

The blessed state is the result of turning to Jesus Christ. Fox meant by turning, one comes to sit under Christ's teaching. Fox used the pair of concepts, "turning to" and "sitting under" Christ's teaching, to describe a single process of movement into the ocean of light. This movement becomes an occasion for learning. By the process of turning to the light, people are delivered into the context for learning immediately from Christ, understandably portrayed by Fox as the inward teacher. This, in fact, is the final aspect of the experience of the light which will be explored. It is the final piece because by learning from Jesus the teacher, people realize that inherent in learning comes an invitation to doing, that is, to ministry. Ministry inevitably carries one beyond oneself and one's relationship with God to an emerging sense of service to God's world and God's children in that world.

At the very heart of Quaker christology, that is, understanding Jesus as the Christ, stands the notion that Christ is one's inward teacher. This is not only a theological understanding, but a spiritual experience. To know the inward Christ by spiritual experience is a life-changing experience. It is not an intellectual wrestling with theological doctrine, but to be met by the inward teacher is to be gracefully grabbed and turned out of the ocean of death and brought to sit in the ocean of life. That is why this learning is life changing. Christ the inward teacher is not a peaceful rabbinic figure solemnity sitting in a temple, but this inward teacher comes in a revolutionary way, often upsetting the tables in the temple! (See Mark 11:15-19 and parallel passages.) This revolutionary work by the inward teacher shows the disciple that "we have this treasure in earthen vessels, to show that the transcendent power belongs to God and not to us." (II Cor. 4:7)

This revolutionary experience of Christ the inward teacher is at the heart of spirituality because the heart is the treasure in each earthen vessel. Fox experientially knew this inward teacher to be the essence of the gospel message. Lewis Benson concludes "in its shortest form, this gospel appeared as the proclamation 'Christ has come to teach his people himself.' This is a kind of symbol...an abridged form of the gospel."[32] To be turned to Christ and sit under his teaching, then, was to be led out of death and given life. In this sense, Quaker spirituality affirms that in experiencing the inward Christ one comes to know him as teacher and guide. In this sense, Quaker spirituality always is educational, *educare* in Latin, meaning "to lead out." The spiritual, educational process commences with God's turning action, realigning spiritually the human heart with the divine source. And with the realignment of turning, the humans are in a place to be taught to live and love, to grow up in relationship with their Lord.

In 1656, Fox traveled to the city of Bristol where he held a meeting on Sunday. Fox began the account telling how he rebuked an evil spirit in a man who was harassing him. He continued:

> And then a glorious peaceable meeting we had, and the word of life was divided amongst them and they were turned from the darkness to the light and to Jesus Christ, their saviour, and the Scriptures were largely opened to them and they turned to the Spirit of God in themselves that would lead them with all truth and open the Scriptures to them.[33]

Fox concluded this meeting with that symbol Benson cited, namely, that Christ "was come to teach people himself."[34]

To begin understanding what Fox meant when he stated that Christ has come to teach his people himself, is the begining to understand something about how Fox wanted humans to live in relationship with God. In the first place, his language is meaningful, as he frequently described relationships with Christ the inward teacher as one in which the disciples' posture is "sitting." In 1655 in London, Fox witnessed a number of people convinced by the Quaker message. He said they "came to be turned to the Lord Jesus Christ, and sat under his teaching and received his power and felt it in their hearts."[35] Just as turning is a classical way of describing the conversion (or convincement) process, so sitting is the Quaker spiritual expression for living in long-term relation with Christ who has turned one. Sitting is a comfortable way to spend time and it connotes "place." One's place is at the feet of the Lord, a real presence who is felt as power in one's heart and heard as word of life in one's ears. As has already been indicated, sitting should not be understood in a passive sense. In fact, with Fox it led to amazing activity in the Spirit. Sitting under Christ's teaching is one's "place," not a "space." It is not confining, but liberating. Christ as teacher does not invite one to a lazy-boy rocker to become spectators to a Christian sport. Rather, it is an invitation to an active life as participants in Christian ministry.

Sitting under Christ's teaching helps one understand what it means to be "under" his teaching. When Christ spoke to Fox's condition, he came up out of the deep, was released from the ocean of darkness and death and freed for relationship with Jesus, his friend. Paradoxically, as Paul stated, this freedom itself is a new bondage. (See for example I Cor. 7:22.) Fox's freedom was a freedom to be "under" the teaching of Christ! In this sense, he became a willing yokefellow, and may well have been influenced by the Matthew passage where Jesus issued the invitation to "come to me, all who labor and are heavy laden, and I will give you rest. Take my yoke upon you, and learn from me, for I am gentle and lowly in heart, and you will find rest for your souls. For my yoke is easy, and my burden is light." (Mt. 11:28-30) To sit under Christ's teaching is to become spiritually yoked to him.

To be yoked with Christ in this way is to be placed into life in such a way to begin the process of learning to live in the Spirit. Contemporarily, Thomas Kelly articulates what it means to sit under Christ's teaching.

> The secret places of the heart cease to be our noisy workshop. They become a holy sanctuary of adoration and of self-oblation, where we are kept in perfect peace, if our minds be stayed on Him who has found us in the inward springs of our life. And in brief intervals of overpowering visitation we are able to carry the sanctuary frame of mind out into the world, into its turmoil and its fitfulness, and in a hyperaesthesia of the soul, we see all mankind tinged with

deeper shadows, and touched with Galilean glories. Powerfully are the springs of our will moved to an abandon of singing love toward God; powerfully are we moved to a new and overcoming love toward time—blinded men and all creation. In this Center of Creation all things are ours, and we are Christ's and Christ is God's. We are owned men, ready to run and not be weary and to walk and not faint.[36]

Kelly points to the culminating feature of learning from the inward Christ: people are moved to an "overcoming love" of God's creatures and God's world. But first, one must immediately learn about God's love for oneself.

Experiencing God's love is the initial turning (conversion) to Christ. One learns more fully and deeply about God's love by sitting under Christ's teaching. Fox described this long-term learning of love as nurture and nourishment. Fox used this sacramental language in the commentary on his ministry in Boston cited earlier.[37] There Fox remarked that those under Christ's teaching were "feeding with his eternal and heavenly food." One aspect of Christ's teaching is to understand it sacramentally, as the bread of life which nurtures the communicant into life eternal (John 6). In a lengthy passage from 1657 on a trip through Wales, Fox gave a glimpse of himself under the burden of Christ's yoke and how through this he was the agent for Christ's feeding.

> And so I passed up to the meeting and stood a-top of a chair about three hours and sometimes leaned my hand off a man's head, and stood a pretty while before I began to speak, and many people sat a-horseback. And at last I felt the power of the Lord went over them all and the Lord's everlasting life and truth shined over all. And the Scriptures were opened to them...and every one of them turned to the light of Christ, the heavenly man, that with it they might all see their sins and see their saviour, their redeemer, their mediator, and feed upon him their bread from heaven.[38]

This sacramental image of Christ as bread from heaven understood Christ as both the source of new life and the nourishment of humans into that life.

Quakers developed their sacramental theology always stating the necessity of an internal spiritual experience. Fox commented on a group of Baptists and Fifth-Monarchy adherents, who prophesied that Christ's return to begin his millenarian reign would literally happen in 1656. Fox retorted:

> And they looked upon this reign to be outward, whenas as he was come inwardly in the hearts of his people to reign and rule there, these professors would not receive him there. So they failed in their prophecy and expectation, and had not the possession of him. But Christ is come and doth dwell in the hearts of his people and reigns there. And thousands, at the door of whose heart he hath been knocking, have opened to him, and he is come in, and doth sup with them and they with him, the heavenly supper with the heavenly and spiritual man.[39]

These last lines, quoting Revelation 3:20, reaffirm Christ and his followers live in daily spiritual communion which is experienced inwardly as a heartfelt actuality. The reality of that experience is not the ingestion of sacramental wafers but the inward joy, peace and love of Christ's felt presence. In this sense, Fox can boldly proclaim Christ's coming is now! Feeding on Christ, as bread, is to live in his presence and power, and is an aspect of sitting under Christ's teaching. Feeding is teaching which sustains.

In addition to the sacramental, another aspect of sitting under Christ's teaching is the *ethical.* By this Fox meant more than a directional statement when he professed Christ was the way to God. By this inward teaching, people travel the way. By learning, they walk. The inward teacher educates, and leads the way.

Coming to sit under the teaching of Christ involves the ethical by suggesting Christ teaches how to walk the way. By dying to the old self and discovering the new authentic self in relationship with God, people necessarily learn to live afresh. Fox spoke plainly to this when he declared as a response to his ministry at Tetbury near Bristol that:

> ...people were turned to the grace and Truth that came by Jesus in their hearts, which would teach them to deny all manner of ungodliness and worldly lust and would teach them to live soberly and godly in the present world; so that every man and woman might know the grace of God which was sufficient and was saving...So here was their teacher, the

grace of God, that would teach them how to live and what
to deny; that would season their words and establish their
hearts and bring their salvation...[40]

Many other places in Fox's *Journal* and epistles specify the ethical
content. Here Christ the inward teacher brings people into the
condition where that learning is possible. Key is the element of grace.
In fact, the whole process of turning to God and being taught by
Christ, the inward guide, is a process of grace. Learning the ethical
is nothing more than learning how to live in the condition of this
grace. To be ethical is to be grace-ful! Generally, grace means
denying ungodliness. In his book, *Addiction and Grace*, Gerald
May says that "grace is the active expression of God's love. God's love
is the root of grace; grace itself is the dynamic flowering of this love;
and the good things that result in life are the fruit of this divine process."[41] Along with the evangelist John, Fox could say that godliness
is living out Christ's new commandment of love: "A new commandment I give to you, that you love one another; even as I have loved
you, that you also love one another. By this all men will know that
you are my disciples, if you have love for one another." (John 13:34-
35) For John, as for Fox, the ethical was practicing this graceful love.
   Love by definition is specific but not concrete in any particular
context. Prescriptions are not always the way to establish what love
looks like in every particular place. The evangelist John and Fox are
more inclined to be open about what Christ's love looks like as
Christians walk the way. This might set Quakers up for a charge of
being wishy-washy, but in fact Quaker spirituality has developed a
way of talking about and living into God's grace which enables them
to avoid a kind of ethical relativism.
   Indeed, the Quaker conviction of living in the light under Christ's
teaching could not be further from a contemporary, wishy-washy,
"do whatever you want in the name of love" approach. Judgment of
the self—particularly, the old self— was the first purging experience
of ethical learning under Christ's teaching. Hugh Barbour speaks for
our day when he states that "to modern Friends it is startling to find
the inward Light described in terms of such fierce judgment. The
Light that ultimately gave joy, peace, and guidance gave at first only
terror."[42] Barbour continues to analyze why Quakers did not fall prey
to a kind of works righteous, prescriptive, ethical approach. The
reason is precisely rooted in their *experience* of Christ the teacher.
Barbour says that Quakers:

...knew most of the theological devices by which men try to find release from judgment. The simplest is rule - keeping, or legal righteousness, the puritan's unremitting temptation to do good. The Saint's anxiety for righteous, though in theory unnecessary because of predestination, was excused as being eagerness to obey God actively. But Quakers were harsh toward all such Will-works, "and knew that if the rule code is Christian, the chance of keeping it is small. Obedience must be deeper.."[43]

Barbour points to the essential ethical concern of Quakers and, one could argue, for Christians of any denomination. The concern is for obedience. Ethics have to do with the right and the good; but above all, ethics, in this Christian sense, have to do with obedience. Called to sit under Christ's teaching is not to learn rules but *to learn love!*

In this context ethics is more like a dance and less like a recitation. The imagery of dance suggests relation and also, how ethics can be learning how to be grace-ful. To be graceful is to obey what Christ calls one to do. It is to learn his movements. Thomas Kelly characterizes the nature of this movement when he describes holy obedience.

> This is something wholly different from mild, conventional religion which, with respectable skirts held back by dainty fingers, anxiously tries to fish the world out of the mudhole of its own selfishness. Our churches, our meeting houses are full of such respectable and amiable people. We have plenty of Quakers to follow God the first half of the way. Many of us have become as mildly and as conventionally religious as were the church folk of three centuries ago, against whose mildness and mediocrity and passionlessness George Fox and his followers flung themselves with all the passion of a glorious and a new discovery and with all the energy of dedicated lives.[44]

"With all the energy of dedicated lives" aptly captures the essence of life lived in the ocean of light. This energy surges not only through the individual, but flows out to the world in ways that turns others to their inward teacher.

Holy obedience which results in sitting under the teaching of Christ is a transformed life given over (dedicated) to the inward teacher. To dedicate one's life in holy obedience is a natural response to knowing oneself loved by God and alive in the ocean of light. It is from this experience and in this knowledge that Quaker spirituality predictably has led from the inner to the outer journey. From the light within, Friends walk into a world of darkness calling friends-to-be to stop, to look and to listen. Thomas Kelly describes Fox and early Quakers as pilgrims from the inner journey to the outward. "Aflame with the Light of the inner sanctuary, they went out into the world, into its turmoil and its fitfulness, and called men to listen above all to that of God speaking within them, to order all life by the Light of the Sanctuary."[45]

V

A GREAT PEOPLE TO BE GATHERED

As we went I spied a great high hill called Pendle Hill, and
I went on the top of it with much ado, it was so steep; but
I was moved of the Lord to go atop of it; and when I came
atop of it I saw Lancashire sea; and there atop of the hill I
was moved to sound the day of the Lord; and the Lord let me
see atop of the hill in what places he had a great people to
be gathered.[1]

With brevity of words and simplicity of vision, Fox narrated his
foundational experience for mission and ministry. His experience
did not remain merely a privatized hearing in the Lord's presence, but
was foundational for the Quaker vision of ministry arising from their
spirituality. No other passage in Fox's *Journal* holds a more basic
place in the narration of Quaker history. Indeed, traditionally the
origin of Quakerism is dated 1652 when George Fox climbed Pendle
Hill.

The thrilling English Quaker storyteller, Elfrida Vipont Foulds, puts
one dramatically into the scene and into the times. Pendle Hill as
story looms large in Fox's *Journal*; it is a mountain experience in the
book. Foulds says about the actual Pendle Hill, "the traveller cannot
miss Pendle Hill. From every viewpoint it stands out, like some
prehistoric monster brooding over the landscape."[2] Just so, the
spiritual experience of Fox atop Pendle Hill is a kind of "re-

experience," a recurring experience from a timeless God who keeps leading men and women up mountains to disclose the divine's desire for a people to be gathered.

Clearly Fox's calling to Pendle Hill and subsequent vision is not unique as an event. However, it is foundational for the Society of Friends who become one more movement in God's historical quest to bring a people into relationship with their creator and redeemer. Pendle Hill is the Quaker Sinai. George Fox is the Quaker Mosaic figure. Exodus 19 tells the familiar story of Israel's wandering in the wilderness after God had delivered them from bondage in Egypt. Sinai (or Horeb) is called the mountain of God. (Ex. 3:1) There, as Israel is encamped at the base of Horeb, one reads:

> Moses went up to God, and the Lord called to him out of the mountain, saying, "Thus you shall say to the house of Jacob, and tell the people of Israel: you have seen what I did to the Egyptians, and how I bore you on eagles' wings and brought you to myself. Now therefore, if you will obey my voice and keep my covenant, you shall be my own possession among all peoples, for all the earth is mine, and you shall be to me a kingdom of priests and a holy nation." (Exodus 19:3-6)

This foundational experience formed the Jewish and Christian people by establishing the basic sense that by virtue of the covenant with God, we are God's daughters and sons, and God is our God. As God's possession, we constitute a kingdom of saints and, in Fox's words, are a great people being gathered.

Gathering a great people always seems a bit presumptuous — even if it is God's desire and doing. Further, that God frequently chooses to do this divine bidding through one or two people at what, retrospectively, turns out to be a "ripe" time, makes anyone who sees himself or herself as "normal" a bit suspicious. Moses seemed unlikely and Fox, well, at best, a bit crazy. Elfrida Foulds again captures the jaundiced perspective which many today are tempted to view Fox's decision to go for a climb.

> It is difficult for us in modern days to realize what a strange decision this was. Only the good old north-country word "daft" can describe it. It was not just that seventeenth century travellers did not climb hills for fun; to turn aside in order to climb Pendle Hill was deflecting George Fox from the object

of his journey, which was to 'declare truth.' His mission was
to the little towns and villages and isolated farm houses, not
to a bare hilltop haunted by the cry of the peewit and the
rippling call of the curlew.[3]

Fox himself seems to have confirmed that some, indeed, thought him
to be daft. He remarked that "people took me for a mad man and
distracted."[4] To understand the mission and ministry of Quaker
spirituality, one needs to follow that daft man up the hill and uncover
his experience.

The first thing to clarify about Fox's Pendle Hill experience is to
declare what it is not. It emphatically is not Fox's "conversion experience." For too long Quakers were given to believe that Pendle Hill
was Fox's conversion. In fact, the pages of this book by now should
have made clear Fox turned to the Lord long before the 1652 Pendle
Hill ascent. In the culminating years of near despair to 1647, Fox
heard Christ's voice speaking to him. So Pendle Hill is not an account
of the personal conversion of Quakerism's founder.

Rather, Pendle Hill is appropriately the *foundation* of *a movement*
which came to be known as Quakerism. Norman Perrin helps one
understand why Pendle Hill is foundational by using the language of
mythology. Perrin says "the truth is that myths are the narrative expression of the deepest realities of human experience."[5] To see Fox's
language as mythology, describing his deepest reality of experience
on Pendle Hill, enables one to get at the symbolic, spiritual truth of
the event. Otherwise, one has to be content merely to agree that
some daft man climbed a hill in a weakened condition and halluci-
nated.

Actually, the Pendle Hill experience is the mythological narration
of a *commissioning*. Far from being a conversion story, it already
presupposed a person opened and in tune with God. It was an
account of Fox's direct and distinctive commissioning to be God's
agent in gathering a great people. Atop Pendle Hill, Fox was given
a mission—to serve God in gathering a great people.

At one level, Friends have been in error to interpret Fox's Pendle
Hill experience as the beginning of the Quaker movement. Insofar
as Quakerism became sectarian, Pendle Hill is the mythological
account of its origin. However, it seems clear Fox was responding
to God's call to help gather a great people who would be more than
a sectarian group called Friends; in fact, one more time in history, he
was called to establish the Christian church, the church universal.

After more than three centuries that this has become the story of another Christian sect may be due more to a blurring of vision and loss of courage than anything else. The spirituality of Fox and early Quakers was not a limiting, sectarian confinement. It was and remains a revival of primitive Christianity understood as the freedom found by people living the fresh winds of the Spirit.

Seen in this light, Pendle Hill is a *pentecostal* experience. It is nothing less than a new Pentecost. In the New Testament, Pentecost is the founding of the Christian church. Acts 2:1-13 narrates how the Spirit is poured out on those assembled, thus fulfilling the promise made by the risen Lord that "you shall receive power when the Holy Spirit has come upon you; and you shall be my witnesses in Jerusalem and in all Judea and Samaria and to the end of the earth." (Acts 1:8) Pentecost fulfills experientially Jesus' promise. But what is often forgotten in the celebration of this pentecostal event is that the Holy Spirit was given for a purpose—that the disciples be witnesses. Inherent in the proper interpretation of Pentecost is the call to *mission* and dedication to *ministry*. The response to Pentecost is predictable; people are turned to the Lord and included in the church, the visible body of Christ.[6]

If rightly understood as a renewing of Pentecost, then one should expect the experience of Fox at Pendle Hill to share common features with the earlier ecclesiastical foundation. A continuation of the giving of the law at Sinai is found in the New Testament account of the gift of the Holy Spirit. Known well is the speaking in tongues associated with Christian Pentecost, but easily forgotten is the awe-ful scene of Moses and the people of Israel before Sinai. Moses brought the people to the foot of the mountain which "was wrapped in smoke, because the Lord descended upon it in fire...and the whole mountain quaked greatly. As the sound of the trumpet grew louder and louder, Moses spoke, and God answered him in thunder."(Exodus 19:18-19) The account then, continues, with the giving of the ten commandments and other laws.

The continuation from Sinai to Pentecost to Pendle Hill is that one man or group received from God immediately the means to life (law/spirit) and the commission to share it with others. In the last chapter, Fox spoke of Christ the inward teacher. He understood that sounding the day of the Lord would bring judgment to the fore and provide the occasion for his ministry of turning people to the Lord. In his own experience, this turning to the Lord would result in others coming to sit under Christ's teaching.

After descending Pendle Hill, Fox spent the night in an alehouse where he and others (he uses the plural, "we") consider the nature of this mission. Fox reported they wrote a paper:

> ...concerning the day of the Lord and how Christ was come to teach people himself by his power and spirit and to bring them off all the world's ways and teachers to his own free teaching, who had bought them and was the Saviour...And the Lord opened to me at that place, and let me see a great people in white rainment by a river's side coming to the Lord...[7]

Fox was revelationally convinced the Lord was about a fresh gathering of the Lord's people. Quaker spirituality was not a sectarian response to some spiritual seepage. Rather, it was pentecostal obedience to a spiritual flood which overcame the old and replanted the new. At Sinai the mountain quaked; in Jerusalem people spake; on Pendle Hill, there were fresh winds of the Spirit. Throughout centuries of religious history symbolic value has been placed on the mountain or high place as a place for meeting or being with the divinity. One need not trace that history for an understanding of Fox's spirituality. What is significant, however, is that this symbolism comes to speak a truth for Fox. In this sense, Pendle Hill is merely one of many occasions in which Fox experienced God and God's call "on the mountain." For example in 1657, he was travelling through Wales and came to Machynlleth. In words reminiscent of the Pendle Hill experience five years earlier, Fox notes he:

> ...came a-top of a hill which they say was two or three miles high. And on this hill-side I could see a great way: and I was moved to sound the day of the Lord there; and set my face several ways and told John ap John, a faithful Welsh minister, in what places God would raise up a people to set under his teaching.[8]

What begins to emerge as the essence of this mountain-top spirituality is not that one meets God on a high hill, but that meeting and living with God puts one on top of all!

Indeed, in many places Fox employs this symbolism of "atop" to indicate how the ocean of light brings one up out of the ocean of darkness and sets one a-top of it. This rearranging in the lives of people, Fox included in words about his ministry in Reading in 1658. Speaking of the political turmoil between the death of Cromwell and the resumption of the monarchy with Charles II, Fox saw this as the hand of God and commented to that end.

> So with heart and voice praise the name of the Lord, to whom it doth belong being on them a-top, and over all hath the supreme. And the nations will he rock, being on them a-top.
>
> And in my great sufferings and travails at Reading I was burdened and almost choked with their hypocrisy and treachery, and falseness, I saw God would bring that a-top of them, which they had been a-top of; and all that must be brought down to that which did convince them, before they could get over that bad spirit within and without: for it is the pure, invisible spirit, that doth and must work down all deceit in people.[9]

From these words one can understand that spiritually the whole process of conversion—turning—is a process of being "turned upside down." One is put atop of the darkness and the old self. In fact, this brings an organizing metaphor for Quaker spirituality: Quaker spirituality is getting on top of things!

From on top of things, spiritually speaking, Fox could discern how others were down under, oppressed by that weight of old self over which he now had come to be. Fox knew:

> ...by this true spirit, in which the true sighing is, I saw over the false sighings and groanings. And by this invisible spirit I discerned all the false hearing and the false seeing and the false smelling which was atop, above the Spirit, quenching and grieving it; and that all they that were there were in confusion and deceit, where the false asking and praying is, in deceit, and atop in that nature and tongue that takes God's holy name in vain, and wallows in the Egyptian sea...[10]

Early on Fox was laying out a blueprint for his ministry which was focused and commissioned afresh with God's Spirit. Indeed, in essence, Quaker spirituality recognizes that by God's Spirit one is led to the mountain top with God and there is commissioned to bring others. As Fox himself declared, "they that walk in this light come to the mountain of the house of God established above all mountains, and to God's teaching, who will teach them his ways."[11]

To come to the mountain house of God is not only to come to be in the presence of the Lord but to join the assembly of those who are the Lord's — to be a part of a great people gathering. When one comes spiritually to be atop of it, one moves into the realm of ecclesiology, the area which deals with the church understood as the body of Christ. Nobody more than Friends has stressed that the *ecclesia*, the church, is a body of people and not a building. The root meaning of *ecclesia* is in the verb, *klesia* (to call) and is directed by a preposition, *ek* (out); hence, the *ecclesia* is a people "called out." In a message to his hearers at Sedbergh in 1652, Fox straightforwardly declared:

> The Lord Christ Jesus was come to teach his people himself and bring them off all the world's ways and teachers to Christ, their way to God; and I laid open all their teachers and set up the true teacher, Christ Jesus...So I opened to the people that the ground and house was no holier than another place, and that the house was not the church, but the people which Christ is the head of...[12]

From these words one can understand the Quaker interpretation of the gathering place for worshippers as simply a "meeting house."

In fact, the meetinghouse is relatively unimportant in the Quaker understanding of the church. Rather, the "place" of action is in the hearts of the women and men turned to Christ and taught by him. It is this which leads Douglas Steere to remark that "the corporate meeting for worship is the ground of Quaker spirituality that undergirds nearly all that Quakers do."[13] It is in the corporate meeting for worship that one comes to the theological intersection where christology, anthropology, and ecclesiology impact and affect one another. In the language of spirituality, this is where the vitalizing, nurturing presence of the Lord (christology) continues to affect the hearts of human beings (anthropology) by knitting them together into a unified witness to the world (ecclesiology). In the earlier chapters both the role of Christ and the response of humans to the christological action were examined. It is time now to pursue the founding of Christ's church, visibly represented by the corporate meeting for worship. Indeed, as Steere remarks, this is the ground of Quaker spirituality because the meeting for worship is the mountain house of God — at least on earth, in time.

Quaker ecclesiology, that is, "doctrine of the church," is nothing more than a restatement of the biblical notion that the church is not a place, but is God's people, a people called out and in the process of being gathered. Early in his ministry when asked by a priest what the church was, Fox responded by saying "the Church was the pillar and ground of Truth, made up of living stones, living members, a spiritual household which Christ was the head of..."[14] Early Quaker spirituality did not concern itself with the establishment of an institutional grouping of people based initially on doctrine and right practice. Rather, Quaker spirituality began with the experience of the living God answering through Christ Jesus the spiritual malaise, depression and alienation of humanity. To those who were "as-if-dead," they were recreated by Christ the foundation of the church to be living stones joined to the spiritual household being erected. These Fox called "living members." They were not living because, physiologically, they are converting oxygen into life, but because the Spirit had been breathed in them. They experienced inclusion into this pentecostal gathering as the risen Lord personally "breathed on them, and said to them, "Receive the Holy Spirit." (John 20:22) They became "members," not because they joined a group (sociology) but because they received the Spirit of the risen Christ (spirituality). As Fox stated it, "the church is the people whom God has purchased with his blood..."[15]

The church is the result of a God who ironically shared life by dying so that the beloved creatures might become living members through this divine love. Fox knew "members of the church" became living only because of the inclusive "work of God" — a work of love— and became members one with another (ecclesiology) only by being "worked over." In offering spiritual advice, Fox wrote in an epistle dated 1656:

> These are members of the Church who know the work in the operation and feeling and come to be members one of another. They who come to the Church that is in God and Christ, must come out of the state that Adam is in...[16]

So, members of a church are nothing more than a people, and "the people are God's house and dwelling."[17] Knowing what (who) the church is, one can understand what goes on in that meetinghouse!

Moving into an understanding of what goes on in the meetinghouse is aided by the provocative words of a Catholic, Rosemary Haughton.

She has written that:

> At all times in its past history, when the wealth and smugness
> of the Church led to revolt and schism, a few people have
> known what it was all about and have come together in their
> response to the poor Christ. These lovers of God saved the
> Church; in a sense they *were* the Church. The mendicant
> orders, the Jesuits, the Quakers, the Salvation Army—there
> have never been very many, but in their poverty Christ died
> and the Church, his body, rose again.[18]

Quakers would probably never think to put themselves in to this
strange company of *militia Christi*, soldiers of Christ. And yet, even
stranger it seems, is to see Quakers as mendicants, that is, a poor one,
a beggar. Mendicants in the minds of most of us conjures up a
Franciscan or some other monkish figure who has taken the vows of
poverty, chastity and obedience. Where does this touch a Quaker
cord and, particularly, point to Haughton's truth that these groups
were the church?

One can know one is edging to the truth rather than pursuing a
dead end by recognizing how closely to the heart of the monastic
spirit Quaker spirituality is. In her book, *Fullness of Life*, Margaret
Miles recognizes the context for monasticism which could also refer
to Quakerism when she remarks "monastic life, then, was a counter
culture."[19] Although one obviously must be careful in assuming a co-
ordination between monasticism and Quakerism (clearly they differ
with regard to the vow of celibacy), nevertheless there are some
distinctive corollaries. Miles says by taking the vows, the monk
"rejects the deadening agenda of secular culture."[20] This is precisely
the place where the monastic spirit touches the harmonious chord in
the Quaker meeting for worship.

The gathered Friends meeting is the place where the deadening
agenda of secular culture is either abandoned or transformed. More
like the Jesuit and Salvation Army pilgrims, and less like the earlier
monks, Quakers have not walked away from secular culture. Rather,
as children of the light, they purposely remain in secular culture to
be a witness to the light and, thereby, be God's sacramentalizing
agents. In the British sense, Quakers are non-conformists. In the
biblical sense, they are leaven. In spiritual categories, they are
obedient. In the worldly, secular sense, they are poor. In this poverty
they shine forth and the world sees Christ's death and resurrection

and knows the beatitude of poverty. God's covenantal call to blessing is always an ironical call to this poverty, to become poor in spirit. In this poverty one finds richness! In the confidence of this richness Quakers were undaunted by a culture which persecuted and oppressed them. In the face of this, Fox stridently encouraged his comrades.

> The Seed is above all. In it walk, in which ye all have life...though the waves of storms be high, yet your faith will keep you to swim above them, for they are but for a time, and the Truth is without time. Therefore keep on the mountain of holiness, ye who are led to it by the light where nothing shall hurt.[21]

It is because Fox and his friends have been brought to the mountain of holiness that they are a gathered people. As a gathered people they are safe and protected. But, ironically, with this security came both a sense of mission and a calling to ministry in a dangerous world! This, then, is what those "poor in the spirit" (Mt. 5:3) are seeing and doing in that meetinghouse.

Remember, the meetinghouse is that mountain house of God where the divinity has graciously sequestered its place in human hearts—or better, has transformitively displaced them from the ocean of darkness. To come up on the mountain is to be able to see the mission—to gather in God's name a great people—and to do ministry, to serve those who are gathered and are being gathered. Fox alludes to both mission and ministry when he described his vision during a time of suffering in 1671.

> And I had a vision about the time that I was in this travail and sufferings, that I was walking in the fields and many Friends were with me, and I bid them dig in the earth, and they did and I went down. And there was a mighty vault top-full of people kept under the earth, rocks, and stones. So I bid them break open the earth and let all the people out, and they did, and all the people came forth to liberty; and it was a mighty place. And when they had done I went on and bid them dig again. They did, and there was a mighty vault full of people, and I bid them throw it down and let all the people out, and so they did. And I went on again and bid them dig again, and Friends said unto me, 'George, thou finds out all things,'

and so there they digged, and I went down, and went along the vault; and there sat a woman in white looking at time how it passed away. And there followed me a woman down in the vault, in which vault was the treasure; and so she laid her hand on the treasure on my left hand and then time whisked on a pace; but I clapped my hand upon her and said, 'Touch not the treasure.' And then time passed not so swift.[22]

This is a powerful statement about the *mission* to which Fox and Friends are called: to gather a great people. It is also a statement of *ministry*: to gather this people means, first of all, going to the place where the people are.

This vision is so compelling because it declares the mission and ministry of the children of the light will "repeat," in one sense, the experience of those who have been liberated. To comment on this in some detail will be, simultaneously, to comment on the nature of the Quaker mission as Fox saw it. Interestingly enough, this vision has Fox walking in the fields. This is reminiscent of his period of despair, except one very important difference. Now he is not alone; he is accompanied by many Friends. In fact, this is the first notation which can be made about the ecclesiological mission—*we go together.* To be in the *ecclesia*, the church, is to be with friends and not be alone. That does not mean one never gets lonely or does not receive particular ministries to do by oneself. But one is not alone again in this world and one need never be lonely.

The second feature emerging from this passage is the very heart of the mission itself—the understanding that the mission is the gathering of a great people. In the context of this mission vision, the gathering will be a *liberation.* In fact, those who will be brought into relationship with God and with the friends of God will be brought up out of the "earth," up out of bondage into the fresh spiritual air and divine light. Fittingly, Fox's first comment upon completing his narration of this vision was to warn "they that can read these things must have the earthly, stony nature off them."[23]

This stony nature was simply one more way of talking about the ocean of darkness and death, a way of talking about pre-conversion bondage. The mission of Quakers is to be christological agents of liberation. Walking in the light enables them to walk down into that dark, binding, hard, drowning place and, in the words of Jesus of Nazareth, "to proclaim release to the captives and recovering of sight to the blind, to set at liberty those who are oppressed." (Luke 4:18)

In the language of the Psalms, they are to be delivered from the pit and brought under the wings of God. As Walter Brueggemann puts it, "expressing one's trust in God's sheltering wings is a bold assertion that the power of the pit has been broken. Imaginative speech may outdistance actual circumstance. But it is a first gesturing of transformed circumstance."[24] It is precisely this transforming work of breaking the power of the pit which describes the mission aspect of Quaker spirituality.

Fox and friends began the mission with a two-fold process. The initial step was to dig. From the perspective of the disciple or believer, this is to "make an opening." Indeed, it is an exciting insight to realize how appropriate the Quaker language of opening is. It functions "on both sides" —for the non-believer (unconverted) and the believer (the transformed one). For the one being transformed or liberated, the opening happens to "us." In this sense, the grammatical voice of opening is *passive*. For those transformed, who are God's agents in digging, they are, in fact, the "openers" to others. Here the grammatical voice is *active*. As missionary agents, Friends now become Christ's revealers and God's disclosers. This is done first, by digging into that place where the trapped and oppressed are bound.

The second step in that process is actually to go down into that place which the digging opened! As Fox said, "I went down." This is mission actualized. Ironically, the believing missionary is called to do exactly what Christ the teacher did: to put himself or herself "in the place" of the one who has not yet seen the light or whose condition has not been spoken to. The one who has been brought a-top will be called in Christ's name to go back down, to go under again and again. In this missionary activity of going down, there is a "breaking out." And it is only when there is a breaking out a great people can be gathered which is, as it develops, the primary mission of Quaker spirituality.

People are enabled to break out because there is a breaking open of the earth. Obviously, in this vision, the earth is used metaphorically for that condition "under" which people are held captive and from which they need to be liberated. Notice how "hard" the metaphor of oppression is: "earth, rocks and stones." Clearly, this again symbolically describes the nature or condition of those who are in the ocean of darkness and death. But, with this symbolism there is a hardness and rigidity which is present. Further, both metaphors of earth and ocean use the operative preposition "under." Humans need to be brought up out of the earth and ocean. In Fox's vision of mission, this was the missionary task. The mission was to break open the earth. This is a refreshingly new way to see the call to be missionaries!

It is through an opening that the people captive to their own self and in a state of alienation from God can move. Through the opening they can break out. This is a spiritual prison escape which can be cheered by all. With the language of liberty Fox characterized the escape and Fox concluded with the note that the new gathering of liberated people constituted "a mighty place." By this Fox would designate both the great people to be gathered (the church universal) as well as the local congregation or assembly of worshippers. All worshippers are called to be missionaries by going into the prisons of this world in the service of a liberating God.

Before pursuing to its conclusion the implications of this vision, one might wonder why this "mighty place" describes the great people gathered in worship. Seeing this "earthy nature" as a statement of human condition comes from Fox's words describing the ministry he and Edward Edwards had in 1657 at Lampeter (Wales). Fox declared "a good service we had for the Lord. The life of Christianity and the power of it tormented the chaffy natures and exceedingly came over them, and some there were reached and convinced."[25] Years later (1669) in Ireland, Fox used similarly moving language when he said "so next day we came to the place of meeting, where we had a brave meeting in the power of God. Oh, the brokenness and life that flowed!"[26] Fox consistently used the language of meeting described adjectivally as mighty, brave, precious, powerful and blessed. Meeting is that "place" figuratively and literally, where liberated individuals gather in the power and blessings of God. It was to the multiplication of those numbers that Fox and friends are called.

Returning to the vision, is the realization that the mission was not a quick job. In fact, there were many people in the grips of this earthly nature which required much digging; indeed, one can know that the ingathering of the saints happens after extensive, arduous digging. So it is that Fox bid them to dig again! And as they commenced, there is a "mighty vault full of people" who need released and that release was going to require some form of gracious intervention. Typically, this intervention is of a cataclysmic, almost apocalyptic variety. In the face of this vault Fox admonished the diggers to "throw it down" and let the people escape.

In the final scene of the mission vision, Fox again had his friends digging and, once more, he went down along the vault. There he encounterd a woman dressed in white. She observed how time was passing away. There are many options for interpretation here, but the clue is to remember the crucial role apocalyptic theology plays in constructing early Quaker spirituality. In all likelihood this woman represented either the church or an angelic figure. Biblically, "the church" (the word in Greek is feminine) is portrayed as a woman. This entire passage may, in fact, be informed by Revelation 12. The initial verses narrate a vision of how the woman (church) delivers her child (the people of God).

> And a great portent appeared in heaven, a woman clothed
> with the sun, with the moon under her feet, and on her head
> a crown of twelve stars; she was with child and she cried out
> in her pangs of birth, in anguish for delivery. (Rev. 12:1-2)

Obviously in this biblical vision, the child can be seen as Jesus Christ or his people. The allusion to Jesus is clear in 12:5 which reads that "she brought forth a male child." One reads further of a church under persecution because when the child is taken to heaven (resurrection) "the woman fled into the wilderness, where she has a place prepared by God, in which to be nourished for one thousand two hundred and sixty days." (Rev. 12:6) John understands the church as the woman in a hostile world and perhaps, this clarity informed Fox in his vision of people trapped in a vault.

Alternatively, the woman could represent an angelic figure and be closer to the theme of the resurrection itself, as a key to release/ rebirth. In this setting it would not be unreasonable to see the visit of the women to the tomb on Easter morning. In Mark's version, the women enter the tomb (representing the place of death and darkness, such as the vault which Fox metaphorically entered) and "they saw a young man sitting on the right side, dressed in a white robe." (Mark 16:5) The correlation of tomb/vault and death/trapped is suggested here.

In Fox's vision, he was followed into the tomb by a second woman who touched the treasure (the people trapped) which made time speed up. This alarmed Fox because he was under missionary compulsion to release the captives before the end of time. In fact, this second woman was restrained and this slowed down time. In this slowing down of time, Fox and friends were able to do their work digging and releasing. In their own way, all missionaries will be called to go for a walk in the fields and dig; they will descend to the vault to be God's gracious assistants for releasing and gathering.

There are correlations between how George Fox and the Apostle Paul received their sense of mission. Paul declared "I did not receive it from man, nor was I taught it, but it came through a revelation of Jesus Christ." (Galatians 1:12) Using Quaker spirituality terminology, Paul had an "opening" which resulted in a mission by which he was "entrusted with the gospel to the uncircumcised." (Gal. 2:7) In Pauline spirituality, one who responds to this gospel is justified and led by the Spirit. To quote Paul, "all who are led by the Spirit of God are sons of God." (Romans 8:14)[27] Fox continued to be vastly influenced by the Pauline sense of mission.

This is no more clearly seen than in an extended passage from 1648, soon after Fox launched his travels in God's service. Notice the use of language associated with Quaker spirituality but in an obvious Pauline context.

> Now I was sent to turn people from darkness to the light that they might receive Christ Jesus, for to as many as should receive him in his light, I saw that he would give power to become the sons of God, which I had obtained by receiving Christ. And I was to direct people to the Spirit that gave forth the Scriptures, by which they might be led into all Truth, and so up to Christ and God, as they had been who gave them forth. And I was to turn them to the grace of God, and to the Truth in the heart, which came by Jesus, that by this grace they might be taught, which would bring them into salvation, that their hearts might be established by it, and their words might be seasoned, and all might come to know their salvation nigh. For I saw that Christ had died for all men, and was a propitiation for all, and had enlightened all men and women with his divine and saving light, and that none could be a true believer but who believed in it. I saw that the grace of God which brings salvation, had appeared to all men, and that the manifestation of the Spirit of God was given to every man to profit withal. These things I did not see by the help of man, nor by the letter, though they are written in the letter, but I saw them in the light of the Lord Jesus Christ, and by his immediate Spirit and power, as did the holy men of God, by whom the Holy Scriptures were written. Yet I had no slight esteem of the Holy Scriptures, but they were very pre-

cious to me, for I was in that spirit by which they were given forth, and what the Lord opened in me I afterwards found was agreeable to them. I could speak much of these things and many volumes might be written, but all would prove too short to set forth the infinite love, wisdom, and power of God, in preparing, fitting, and furnishing me for the service he had appointed me to; letting me see the depths of Satan on the one hand, and opening to me, on the other hand, the divine mysteries of his own everlasting kingdom.[28]

The primary mission Fox described has two features. The first is to *turn* people to the same Christ Jesus who speaks to the condition of every person. The second feature is to *direct* people to the guidance of the Spirit. These two features are the keys to the mission and ministry as Quaker spirituality both experiences and articulates them. Turning is the specific focus for the Quaker apostolic mission. Directing is the particular guiding image of Quaker ministry.

This quotation which details God's mission to Fox, as he understood it, provides the content for the more general Pendle Hill vision. To be turned is already understood in conversion/transformation language. In typically Johannine fashion, Fox asserted that anyone who receives Christ Jesus will be given the power to become a child of God. Interestingly at this juncture, Fox revealed the real key to his qualification to be God's missionary. He did what God called him to do because he had already experienced what God is going to do and can offer release to those captive in their earthy vaults! In speaking about becoming an adoptive child, Fox knew about it experientially because adoption is that "which I had obtained by receiving Christ."

To turn people from darkness to light is to turn them to God's grace—their salvation. This mission introduces an experience, not right doctrine. The missionary enterprise of Fox and Quakers was to "move" people, to turn them, to displace them. The missionary thrust digs into and enters people's earthy places and breaks those open. This means the missionary work of turning people to the light of Christ is not always perceived as pleasant!

Fox paid a price for being Christ's apostolic emissary. Just how steep it was can be seen in his words as a result of his preaching at Mansfield in 1649.

When the priest had done I declared the Truth to the priest

and people. But the people fell upon me with their fists, books, and without compassion or mercy beat me down in the steeplehouse and almost smothered me in it, being under them...They put me in the stocks and brought a whip to whip me, but did not. And as I sat in the stocks they threw stones at me, and my head, arms, breast, shoulders, back and sides were so bruised that I was mazed and dazzled with the blows.[29]

There is a burden which goes with one's mission. Only because Fox felt himself clearly called and powerfully in the Spirit could he answer the call and walk in the Spirit. In his eloquent words, God had been present "in preparing, fitting, and furnishing me for the service he had appointed me to." This time of preparation is pursued in the next chapter on ministry in God's Spirit.

But now, Fox concludes the development of his sense of mission. After stating his apostolic commission was to turn people to the light, Fox followed with an even more detailed description of what that meant.

Now, when the Lord God and his son, Jesus Christ, did send me forth into the world, to preach his everlasting gospel and kingdom, I was glad that I was commanded to turn people to that inward light, spirit, and grace, by which all might know their salvation, and their way to God; even that divine Spirit which would lead them into all Truth and which I infallibly knew would never deceive any. But with and by this divine power and spirit of God, and the light of Jesus, I was to bring people off from all their own ways to Christ, the new and living way, and from their churches, which men had made and gathered, to the Church in God, the general assembly written in heaven, which Christ is the head of, and off from the world's teachers made by men, to learn of Christ, who is the way, the truth and the life...[30]

Once more, Fox restated his apostleship — the Lord "sent" him into the world. Interestingly, Fox used another familiar Quaker phrase to describe his work: his mission was to preach the everlasting gospel which is the kingdom of God.

The preaching of the gospel was the key to Fox's mission and defined his ministry. As Lewis Benson remarked, "the gospel he [Fox] preached was the foundation of everything he taught and everything he did."[31] Benson was cited earlier saying, "in its shortest form, this gospel appeared as the proclamation 'Christ has come to teach his people himself.' This is a kind of symbol — an abridged form of the gospel."[32] Fox closely linked mission and ministry. Mission is the task or commission to a vision; in this case, the mission was to preach the gospel which brought people to sit under the teaching of the inward Christ. Ministry is the actual carrying out of the mission—the doing of the task and actualizing the vision. Fox directed people to this inward light, spirit, and grace by coming to Christ, one's inward teacher.

Knowing this inward Christ is salvation and realizes one's way to God. Salvation is to know through experience a great people gathered. In this sense Quaker spirituality is essentially "evangelistic" and its mission is a call to evangelize the world. Fox and early Friends had no desire to make everyone Quakers; rather, their mission was to help God gather everyone into God's kingdom. In this they are truly inclusive and essentially universalistic! Quaker spirituality appropriately sees universal evangelicalism as rooted in an experience of the inward Christ who gathers his people.

There are various ways of describing the experience of the inward Christ. Hugh Barbour writes that "Friends spoke of Light, the Spirit, and Christ within so interchangeably that no uniform distinction can be made clear..."[33] The inward Christ is light. Spiritually speaking, the light is the necessary means to "see," and shows men and women both where they are (sin) and where they are going (salvation). Without this light, humanity is blind and ignorant. The aspect of ministry which turns people to that inward light puts them in a place where they see and know.

Fox is quite clear this light is not ours as a natural gift. In a debate with John Owen, vice-chancellor of Oxford, and Oliver Cromwell, Fox told Cromwell that the light "was divine and spiritual from Christ the spiritual and heavenly man, which was called the life in Christ, the Word and the light in us."[34] It is, no doubt, more properly spoken to say one *participates* in this inward light than that one has it. This language of participation points to the third aspect of the inward Christ, namely, that one has this Christ (light) by grace. Grace is a freely given gift of God. A significant feature of the ministry of Fox was to turn people to this gift of God which was already available, already there! In the light, individuals could see and feel the gifts of life which God had already freely given. This life was the "life of

Christ" which is ours when we come up out of the ocean of death into the light which overcomes the darkness.

Grace is a word often carelessly used in our own contemporary culture. As Thomas Merton warns, even those who retain a religious dimension to the word find it easy to misuse. Merton says:

> We are so accustomed to talking about the 'state of grace' and 'degrees of grace' that we come to imagine that grace is some kind of 'thing' or commodity, like oxygen or gasoline.
>
> We are almost in the habit of treating grace as something that fills up a tank in our soul and keeps us going like supernatural fuel.[35]

Merton focuses on what Fox wanted to communicate when he said his mission was to turn people to that inward grace. Merton affirms "grace is simply the intensity and vitality of our life in God. It is a special quality of soul resulting from the radiation of the divine life in us, and from the presence of God in us."[36] Experientially, the affective sense of knowing this inward grace puts one in a place to feel "more alive, more vital." Obviously, one can feel alive without God's Spirit, but the inward Spirit enables individuals to feel vital. What's more, this vitality lasts a life-time; indeed, ironically the believer will feel vital even through the experience of death. This is what makes God's Spirit different than drugs, which deaden or induce particular feelings.

The feeling of vitality coming from the experience of grace means individuals have found and are in touch with the Spirit. Once more, Fox acknowledged that a part of his ministry in fulfillment of his mission was to turn people to this inward Spirit. This Spirit, like light and grace, is not the "human spirit," as we might suspect. It is the Spirit of God/Christ, the divine presence. In Greek, the word for "spirit" (pneuma) is also translated "wind." To be in touch with the Spirit is like being in the wind; one feels and knows it without seeing it or capturing it.

Thomas Kelly describes the "sense of Presence," and defines the Quaker understanding of turning to the Spirit.

> The sense of Presence is as if two beings were joined in one single configuration, and the center of gravity is not in us but in that Other. As two bodies, closely attached together and whirling in the air, are predominantly determined by the

heavier body, so does the sense of Presence carry within it a sense of our lives being in large part guided, dynamically moved from beyond our usual selves. Instead of being the active, hurrying church worker and the anxious, careful planner of shrewd moves toward the good life, we become pliant creatures, less brittle, less obstinately rational. The energizing, dynamic center is not in us but in the Divine Presence in which we share.[37]

Fox's mission in calling a great people to be gathered turned people within to themselves to discover this sense of Presence, the light of Christ. This sense of Presence simùltaneously is experienced as our Center. In an ironic fashion, the one who turns "inward" to discover this Divine Presence will, in fact, go "out of" himself or herself. Paul Tillich helps in understanding this basic *ecstatic* dimension of becoming centered in God's Spirit.

If the divine Spirit breaks into the human spirit, this does not mean that it rests there, but that it drives the human spirit out of itself. The "in" of the divine Spirit is an "out" for the human spirit. The spirit, a dimension of finite life, is driven into a successful self-transcendence; it is grasped by something ultimate and unconditional..."Ecstasy" is the classical term for this state of being grasped by the Spiritual Presence.[38]

Fox did not use the classical language of spirituality (ecstasy) to describe experiencing this spiritual presence. Instead, he spoke about centering and sitting under the teaching of the inward Christ. This seems to be even more appropriate spiritual language for today's world than the language of ecstasy.

As Fox turned people to the inward Christ, they came to know this divine Spirit as their salvation. In Fox's language, he brought people to "the new and living way," into integrity and wholeness—a context to feel fully alive and know fully the purpose and meaning in life. This experience of the inward light, spirit and grace Fox suggests as undergoing an experience of baptism. For him baptism has less to do with getting wet than *being turned.* So Fox could say in Paul's words, now "we too might walk in newness of life." (Rom. 6:4)

Fox pursued the spirituality of Romans when Paul wrote sacramentally about the circumcision of the spirit. Paul argued in Romans that the real Jew was the one who, indeed, had been circumcised, but circumcised by the spirit rather than the knife.

> For he is not a real Jew who is one outwardly, nor is true
> circumcision something external and physical. He is a real
> Jew who is one inwardly, and real circumcision is a matter
> of the heart, spiritual and not literal. (Rom. 2:28-29)

Quaker spirituality contends the sacramental experience is inaugu-
rated by turning to the inward Christ. The experience of the living
Christ is a spiritual, cardiac circumcision which brings people off the
old ways and enables them to emerge from this transforming
operation to live fresh and new in the covenantal relationship with
God. What Fox said about training children applies to all "new-
borns" in the Spirit.

> ...so all Christians, and all that made a profession of
> Christianity, ought to train up their children and servants in
> the new covenant of light...And they ought to train them up
> in the law of life, the law of the Spirit, the law of love and
> of faith, that they might be made free from the law of sin and
> death. And all Christians ought to be circumcised by the
> Spirit, which puts off the body of the sins of the flesh, that
> they may come to eat of the heavenly sacrifice, Christ Jesus,
> that true spiritual food, which none can rightly feed upon but
> they that are circumcised by the Spirit.[39]

Existence in this new and vital way is life focused on mission,
centered in ministry and nurtured by Christ's spiritual presence and
power.[40] Again, Tillich described in a non-Quaker way what Fox
knew experientially about the spiritual Presence, that "when it grasps
man, it creates unambiguous life."[41] The centered life is the unambiguous life, life lived in power and with meaning. The Quaker spiritual language of an individual rooted and grounded in the inward
light, spirit and grace, also applies and is employed to describe the
corporate gathering—the church—as it endeavors to be gathered and
"covered" by the Spirit present in worship. The experience of the
inward Christ is never an isolated, individual experience among
Friends. The personal experience always leads to the communal.
We have now come full circle. The mission of Fox and that which
describes Quaker spirituality was not to save individual souls, but to
gather a great people. It is to take the whole crowd up the mountain

to be turned to Christ and taught by him. These gathered people are re-established in right relationship with their God and between themselves to be God's great people and Christ will be their all-loving savior. Hear again the words of Fox in Wales (1657) in what amounts to a summary of his mission:

> ...I was moved to declare the Lord had a seed in those places; and after, there has been a brave people raised up in the covenant of God and gathered in the name of Jesus, where they have salvation and free teaching.[42]

A key aspect of Quaker spirituality is this idea that the new covenant formed a new community based on the inward Christ as foundation.

George Fox clearly had been opened to see how the new covenant picked up the Old Testament theme from Jeremiah. Jeremiah was told by the Lord that:

> ...Behold the days are coming, says the Lord, when I will make a new covenant with the house of Israel and the house of Judah...this is the covenant which I will make with the house of Israel after those days, says the Lord: I will put my law within them, and I will write it upon their hearts; and I will be their God, and they shall be my people. (Jer. 31:31-33)

Obviously, the Christian perspective proclaims this new covenant is Jesus Christ and the New Testament is its witness. Fox would agree. But, in his estimation, the power had been eroded and life had left the Christians of his day. His own experience was an immediate, fresh blowing of the Spirit, a rediscovery of the power of Christ's presence and the subsequent commission to gather a great people into that life and power. As Lewis Benson puts it, "Fox in all his work and teaching is trying to gather Friends into a worshipping fellowship that is based on the New Covenant..."[43] It is this new community of transformed men and women which is the great people to be gathered.

The new community founded upon Christ is the place where men and women are empowered and feel life. Obviously, Quaker spirituality does not have a uniqueness in these affections; nevertheless, they are the touchstones that give a sense of the progress to the early Quaker mission. In his own words, Fox stipulated that this work was ongoing.

Thus the work of the Lord went forward, and many were turned from the darkness to the Light within the compass of these three years, 1646, 1647, and 1648. And diverse meetings of Friends, in several places, were then gathered to God's teaching, by his light, spirit, and power; for the Lord's power brake forth more and more wonderfully.[44]

To be called into this power is to be be called into a powerful community. In the words of Thomas Merton, it is a call to be a person of the church, a *vir ecclesiae*. A person of the church is called out of the self as a part of that ocean of death and darkness, and called into a life of holiness, into God's place. For Merton, as for Fox, this holiness has a christological foundation.

Contact with the risen humanity of Christ is true holiness. Growth in holiness is growth in our union with the risen Christ. But Christ lives and acts in His Church. Growth in union with the church, deeper participation in the prayer life of the church, in her sacramental life, in her other activities, gives us a deeper sharing in the life and mind and prayer of Christ Himself.[45]

The mission of Fox, then, was simply the gathering of a great people, the reformation of the *ecclesia*. For him, Christ was the source and resource of people's learning and living in the spiritual center.

In a letter of 1654 to Friends in the ministry, Fox nicely summarized the communal power which united them. He admonished:

Friends everywhere abroad scattered, know the power of God in one another and in that rejoice; for then you rejoice in the Cross of Christ, him who is not of the world, which Cross is the power of God to all them that are saved. So you that know the power and feel the power, you feel the Cross of Christ, you feel the Gospel, which is the power of God unto salvation to everyone that believeth.[46]

To know this power of God in one another is to know the universal loving God at work in the world. This is to know that in being loved, one will be called to go into the world and love!

Rosemary Haughton begins the final chapter of *The Passionate God* by saying that "any book about Christianity must properly be a call to mission, for Christianity is a 'sending out' of people to share the good news that life is possible."[47] Quaker spirituality holds that all Christians will be sent out—in going out in mission they will all be called to particular ministries. In this sense, the life of the Quaker will be the life of imitating Christ. Just as Christ spoke to the condition of Fox, so Fox was called to go into the world "answering that of God" in every person. For every Quaker, and every believer, mission always turns out to be ministry.

VI

WALK CHEERFULLY OVER THE WORLD

Bring all into the worship of God. Plough up the fallow
ground...And none are ploughed up but he who comes to
the principle of God in him which he hath transgressed.
Then he doth service to God; then the planting and the wa-
tering and the increase from God cometh. So the ministers
of the Spirit must minister to the spirit that is transgressed and
in prison, which hath been in captivity in every one; whereby
with the same spirit people must be led out of captivity up
to God, the Father of spirits, and do service to him and have
unity with him, with the Sriptures and one with another. And
this is the word of the Lord God to you all, and a charge to
you all in the presence of the living God, be patterns, be
examples in all countries, places, islands, nations, wherever
you come; that your carriage and life may preach among all
sorts of people, and to them. Then you will come to walk
cheerfully over the world, answering that of God in every
one...[1]

These words of 1656 to Friends in the ministry contain one of the
most oft-quoted phrases from Fox's writing, namely, "to walk
cheerfully over the world, answering that of God in every one." To
understand the feelings and theology contained in this quotation
enables others to comprehend the ministry dimension of Quaker

spirituality. Fox portrays ministry as a movement—a doing. It is not a spiritually sedentary life. Rather, ministry in that light, grace and spirit of Christ causes believers to rise up and walk.

Not only will Christ's servants walk, but they will walk cheerfully. This clarion note of joy characterizes those who are already living in God's kingdom. There are many contemporary examples who assist our understanding of what Fox must have meant. One thinks of Mother Theresa, Dorothy Day or the Peace Pilgrim. Perhaps the least well-known of these three, the Peace Pilgrim, was a contemporary mobile monk until she was killed in 1981. The Peace Pilgrim undertook a ministry literally of walking cheerfully over the world. She spoke eloquently of the simplicity of her detached life, "think of how free I am! If I want to travel, I just stand up and walk away."[2] She points to the maturity of her relationship with God. This maturity has ripened her with the fruits of the Spirit. In the freedom of this she joyfully ministered in the world. She tells the reader:

> To know God is to reflect love toward all people and all creations. To know God is to feel peace within—a calmness, a serenity, an unshakeableness which enables you to face any situation. To know God is to be so filled with joy that it bubbles over and goes forth to bless the world.[3]

It is a lovely and apt image to think of Fox as bubbling over. This is exactly the experiential prod which moved him and us to walk cheerfully.

The mission of Quaker spirituality is defined as gathering a great people. The greatest people would be a global people. This great people to be gathered is not simply English nor seventeenth century. Contemporary Quaker spirituality, as Fox would envision it, would not be an anachronistic attempt somehow to foster a kind of sectarian "Quaker-Amish." In fact, Fox was not even concerned for "Quakers;" his mission was a great people. Against this, one would have to judge contemporary Quakers a spiritual failure!

Quakers have talked theologically in "universal" terms and that has the advantage of being temporally encompassing as well as globally inclusive. The focus in ministry is to "answer" that of God in *every* one. Fox projected that for every one in the world there will be a time experientially when that person will literally or metaphorically hear a voice and know that "there is one, even Christ Jesus, that can speak to thy condition."[4] Then, that person will experience his or her heart leaping for joy just as Fox's did in 1647! Furthermore, it will be out of this joy that each will walk cheerfully into the world of ministry.

Historically, the story of Quaker ministry spreading over the world usually begins with George Fox's travels and, then, takes up the pilgrimages of the "Valiant Sixty" beginning in 1654. The concern in this book is not to recount what the Valiant Sixty did nor their successors among seventeenth century or twentieth century Quakers. Rather, our focus is on the spirituality which issues forth in global, joyful ministry. As John Punshon rightly remarks, "above all, Quakerism was a spiritual and only secondarily an intellectual movement...The most important features of early Quakerism were its missionary endeavour and the persecution it attracted, not its theological novelty."[5] Ministry is a spiritual movement as Quakers both understand and practice it.

Above all, Quakers have sought to understand ministry as the New Testament witness portrays it. Ministry is not something only priests and pastors do, but ministry is what all do who are called to be Christ's disciples. In the biblical sense, ministry is *diakonia*, "service." To translate and, thereby understand, *diakonia* as simply a "deacon" is to misunderstand and malnourish the New Testament understanding of service. The apostle Paul again is the key for understanding of the *ecclesia* (the church) and its ministries. In his initial letter to the church at Corinth, Paul says:

> Now there are varieties of gifts, but the same Spirit; and there are varieties of service (*diakonion*), but the same Lord; and there are varieties of working, but it is the same God who inspires them all in every one. To each is given the manifestation of the Spirit for the common good. (I Cor. 12:4-7)

Paul goes on to enumerate a number of spiritual gifts. Two key observations for the purpose of Quaker spirituality emerge from careful consideration. The first is that Paul, and Fox after him, understood ministries in the plural. There are *varieties* of ministry! Secondly, ministries are rooted in gifts and gifts are nothing but manifestations of God's grace, the *charismata* of God's working in individual lives.

Quaker spirituality holds since there is "that of God in every one," as soon as that of God is "answered," each person becomes not only a disciple, but a minister. A minister is nothing more than a disciple who is serving in the world out of God's gifts. In the company of the great people being gathered, there is a responsible mutuality in the ministry of the all to all. To call it pastoral care can be misleading if the understanding of "pastor" is limited to the person up front. A contemporary, non-Quaker, Scotsman has captured what seems to be the essence of this Quaker vision of ministry when he says:

> Pastoral care is grounded in mutuality, not in expertise; it is possible because we share a common humanity with all the splendor and all the fallibility which that implies...In the last analysis there is no cleverness or accomplishment in pastoral care. It is no more (and no less) than sharing with another in the experience of grace, a surprising, unsought gift.[6]

In the widest, Quaker sense one focus on ministry is pastoral care, the story of persons sharing with one another in the experience of grace! Ministry as pastoral care actually is the exercising of one's gifts. Fox encouraged and enabled ministers to exercise their gifts, in the arena of spiritual direction.

Spiritual direction has a long and storied tradition in the Roman Catholic church. Currently, in the Protestant tradition there has been the concomitant discovery of spiritual direction. Indeed, if pastoral counseling were the rage in seminaries in the 1960's, spirituality and spiritual direction have become "the thing" in the past decade.[7] With recognizing what spiritual direction really is, comes the recognition that Quakers, too, have always been doing it and it occupies an essential place in Quaker spirituality.

A classical, Catholic monastic perspective offered by Thomas Merton describes spiritual direction as:

> ...a continuous process of formation and guidance, in which a Christian is led and encouraged *in his special vocation,* so that by faithful correspondence to the graces of the Holy Spirit he may attain to the particular end of his vocation and to union with God.[8]

Present in Merton's definition are some key terms which characterize spiritual direction as exercised by Quakers in their gifts for ministry. Favored by Quakers is the language of guidance, particularly in the sense of a continuous process, which recaptures the sense of conversion as a life-long process, a being called (*vocatio*) in relationship with God and among the people (*ecclesia*) of God.

A more contemporary as well as more Quakerly understanding of spiritual direction is found in the words of Gerald May when he begins his book on spiritual direction with these words: "The essence of spiritual guidance or direction can be seen whenever one person helps another to see and respond to spiritual truth."[9] May certainly takes spiritual direction out of the ranks of a priestly or professional order and states any one can be a spiritual director to another. The proof of effectiveness is whether the other person sees and responds to spiritual truth. Recognizing that differing traditions focus on either a "master" spiritual director or, at the other end, "simply as an informed human being who represents a channel of grace," May concludes that "in either case it is generally assumed that the 'real' director is the Holy Spirit, manifested through the relationship in a graced way."[10] This becomes very close to what Fox and Quaker spirituality mean when they insist that people must come to sit under the guidance of Christ's teaching. As this is understood comes the appreciation for both what a rich heritage and rich potentiality Quaker spirituality has for spiritual vitality in the twenty-first century!

A very useful resource on spiritual guidance among Friends is found in the 1909 Swarthmore Lecture by William Charles Braith-waite. From it one senses immediately how the initial convincing experience of Christ's action forms the basis of spiritual guidance. Braithwaite stated:

> The Quaker Publishers of Truth told men that doctrine must be transmuted into experience, the Scriptures into words of power, the external institutions of the church into a living fellowship, before they could become food to the soul.[11]

On the superficial level, this does little more than reiterate that experience is primary and foundational for Quaker spirituality and, in turn, is the basis for spiritual guidance. In his own way Braithwaite described the classic Quaker formulation in surprisingly contemporary ways. To document a more recent explanation one can cite the words of Alan Jones saying "the art of spiritual direction is rooted in two basic convictions. The first is that our relationship with God is of primary and fundamental importance...The second is that our relationship with God is bound up with our relationship with one another and with the whole created order."[12] What Jones acknowledges is what every Quaker minister knows, namely, spiritual guidance has both a personal and a corporate dimension. To enter into relationship with God is to enter into covenant with the one who has called us to mature in that relationship with the divine and with those others who also are living in the covenanted bond. Perhaps this is why, finally, in the language of Jones that spiritual guidance is best understood as spiritual friendship! After all, Jesus shared the secret of intimacy with his disciples when he assures them, "No longer do I call you servants," and then promised, "but I have called you friends." (John 15:15)

In the succinct words of Jones, "while I am not always sure I need a director, I do know that I need friends."[13] The key to spiritual friendship, as Quaker spirituality encourages it, is to be in league with a friend(s) who share the experience of the inward light and endeavor to walk and to grow in that light. This is not an automatic nor aimless meandering, but a learning to walk and live in the light as a "work of grace" which requires learning the "art of spiritual direction." A contemporary, Franciscan spiritual director actually defines spirituality as "simply the *art of growing closer to God*."[14] In this sense, spiritual guidance with friends is always dealing with the issues of growth and maturity.

In the language from Braithwaite the spiritually mature (directed/ guided) person has been seen:

> ...to produce a type of character which is probably the chief enrichment of Christianity hitherto made by Quakerism, the man or woman who goes through life endeavoring to decide every question as it arises, not by passion or prejudiced, nor mainly by the conclusions of human reason, but chiefly by reference to the light of God that shines in the prepared soul.[15]

With this image of "the prepared soul" comes the step into the metaphorical world of Quaker spiritual guidance.

This effective metaphor of the prepared soul describes the process of spiritual guidance. First, it recognizes at one time souls are "unprepared." Then, by the conversion through a spiritual guiding process, God prepares the soul. Allowance is also given that a prepared soul could become unprepared if undo attention is not paid to living in the measure of light one has been given. Maturity, in a spiritual, developmental perspective, does not mean one is finished, but rather that one is living "perfectly" in the grace of God. Finally, the idea of a prepared soul is an apt way for Quakers to use the symbolic language of the Seed. This metaphor lends itself splendidly to the process of spiritual guidance. Quakers have a well-developed sense of how the soul is prepared. As usual, it has first and foremost to do with experience, because it is in the experience of God that one comes to know the truth in one's life. Braithwaite sees the process in terms of becoming "sensitized." He wrote:

> It is upon this developed sensitiveness to spiritual light that Friends have always relied as the chief instrument for discerning truth. The sensitiveness was, I think, cultivated by the first Friends mainly in two ways, both of which under the changed condition of our own time still retain all their old value. They sought to make their souls receptive and their vision clear, and, in the second place, they coveted not only a vision, but an experience.[16]

The leading quotation of this chapter looks into what Braithwaite states here about experience. The minister is the one who already experiences the light within, has turned and come to sit under Christ's teaching, and knows the liberation commensurate with that experience. It is in that spirit that Fox says:

> So the ministers of the Spirit must minister to the spirit that is transgressed and in prison, which hath been in captivity in every one; whereby with the same spirit people must be led out of captivity up to God...[17]

This is the beginning of ministry for every one; to have a "visitor" in our prison of transgression.

The initial stage of the ministry of spiritual direction is the "preparation of the seedbed," to use an agricultural metaphor. The person offering spiritual guidance assists the operating light of Christ to begin revealing one's true condition. The words of Fox to a gathering of Ranters at Twycross illustrates spiritual guidance in this preparatory stage.

> ...I was moved in the dread of the Lord to speak to them and reprove them and the Lord's power came over them so as

some of them were reached and convinced and received the
spirit of God and are come to be a pretty people and live and
walk soberly in the Truth of Christ.[18]

To "reach" reveals how the imprisoned spirit is contacted. Spiritual
guidance at this stage is any activity which enables one to "look into"
and, then, "speak to" the condition of the other's imprisoned soul.

What Fox described as the process of reaching the Ranters is
repeated many times as his ministry of preaching includes this initial
phase of spiritual guidance. In a sermon from 1653 Fox said:

And when the people were settled I stood up (on a seat) and
the Lord opened my mouth to declare his everlasting Truth
and his everlasting day, and to lay open all their teachers and
their rudiments, traditions, and inventions that they had been
in, in the night of apostasy, since the apostles' day; and to
turn them to Christ their teacher; and to set up and direct
them to his worship, and where to find the spirit and Truth
that they might worship God in; and opened Christ's
parables to them, and directed them to the spirit of God in
them that would open the Scriptures and parables to them;
and how all might come to know their Saviour and sit under
his teaching and come to be heirs of the kingdom of God,
turning them from the darkness to the light, and the power
of Satan unto God, so that every one might come to know
who their teacher was, Christ Jesus and the Lord God, as the
prophets and the apostles and the true Church did, and so
to know both God and Christ's voice by which they might
see all the false shepherds and teachers that they had been
under and see the true shepherd, priest, bishop, and
prophet, Christ Jesus whom God commanded them to hear.
And largely did I declare the word of life to them for about
three hours time and all was still, and quiet, and satisfied.[19]

A number of spiritual guidance characteristics emerge from this
significant passage. In the first place, Fox clearly attributes his
ministry to the work of the Spirit. He tells us that "the Lord opened
my mouth." This confessional perspective acknowledges he is being
used instrumentally by God. A second and corollary point suggests
Fox is convinced that his words were not mere human words. On
the contrary, he was persuaded that he spoke revelationally! His

words were really God's words; his power and witness really were God's. Hence, when Fox declared that God opens my mouth, he was audaciously but confidently saying that he spoke revelationally and he opened others to God's place and truth. In his work on Fox, Doug Gwyn states:

> Quaker preaching...will be seen to lay primary emphasis upon apocalypse in its literal sense of revelation. Geopolitical speculation gave way to knowledge of Christ's return in personal experience...What we find in Fox's preaching are the same hopes shared by his Puritan contemporaries, yet a new basis for these hopes in a radically personal spirituality.[20]

The new basis for this spirituality is the call to experience, and from that experience, the call to direct others to their own experience of God.

The experiential result of Fox's preaching the everlasting gospel was that people were turned to Christ. Fox explicitly declared that he was "to set up and direct them to his (Christ's) worship," and that he "directed them to the spirit of God in them that would open the Scriptures and parables to them."[21] It is important to note that the spiritual direction offered to people was direction leading to experience rather than merely a cognitive knowledge of scripture.

Quakers understand the primary element of spiritual direction to be *transformational* rather than informational. Gwyn recognizes this when he appropriately wrote "transformation is the ultimate goal of gospel preaching."[22] Preaching is but one aspect of spiritual guidance whose purpose is the transformation of human lives. Through this process transformed people "come to be heirs of the kingdom of God." In the words of Braithwaite:

> It is through men that the Spirit of Christ manifests Himself: this human personality of ours is the divine instrument for the use of the church alike in its work of building up its own numbers, and in its wider service of advancing the kingdom of God.[23]

The ministry of the disciple in his or her transforming work is to prepare the soil of the soul for God's seed.

Farmers know the first step in the agricultural process is to prepare the seedbed. So, too, this is the case for spiritual guidance. The idea of God's seed implanted in each human being is an essential affirmation of the capacity for the divine/human relationship. The most important thing about the image of the seed, as it was with the image of the light within, is clearly to understand the seed is not an innate, natural, human endowment. Rather, the seed is God's gift of the divine presence itself. It is graciously given, not naturally conceived. The seed itself is nothing other than the Word—Christ himself. To have Christ's seed implanted begins the germinating process of spiritual awakening and growth. With care and spiritual nurture this seed bears fruit in our lives. To prepare the soil of our soul puts us in a place to make space for the gift of God's love.

In Fox's ministry of spiritual guidance, he prepared this soil for Christ the seed. Fox told a general meeting of Quakers in 1658 that the fellowship of God's kingdom belongs to them in whom the seed had been planted.

> Then I was moved by the power and spirit of the Lord, to open unto them the promise of God, how that it was made to the Seed, not to seeds, as many, but to one, which Seed was Christ; and that all people, both males and females should feel this Seed in them, which was heir of the promise; that so they might all witness Christ in them, the hope of glory, the mystery which had been hid from ages and generations, which was revealed to the apostles, and is revealed again now, after this long night of apostasy...Now again, the everlasting Gospel must be preached to all nations, and to every creature, that they may come into the pure religion, to worship God in the spirit and in truth, and may know Christ Jesus their way to God, and him to be the author of their faith, and may receive the Gospel from heaven, and not from men; in which Gospel, received from heaven, is the heavenly fellowship, which is a mystery to all the fellowships in the world.[24]

This clear christological basis of the seed is Christ. God's promise is the gospel promise for life and heavenly fellowship. Fox says we can "feel" this seed in us! What can he possibly mean except that sense of *empowering* which believers experience when their souls have been prepared and the seed implanted. It is as if one were able to join mid-west farmers on a hot June evening who comment they can "almost hear the corn growing!" The feel of the seed is a sense of *vitality*, the experience of activity of life. This "feeling" is emphasized in Fox's encounter with Rice Jones in Nottingham. At the conclusion of this encounter Fox acknowledged that some of Jones' followers became convinced and:

...many of them were brought to the Lord Jesus Christ, and were settled upon him, sitting down under his teaching and feeding, where they were kept fresh and green; and the others that would not be gathered to him soon after withered.[25]

The metaphor of the seed is amazingly useful because of its levels of meaning. The seed once planted, because it is an organic metaphor, grows! In its power men and women become the plants into which the seed has grown. In its power they are kept fresh and green! To be outside or alienated from the power of the seed's presence is to wither and live lifelessly. From the preparation of their soul, they now become seedlings in Christ.

As Fox describes some specifics of living in the spirit, he declared this power and life is a calm and cool place. In 1658 he addressed Friends in the ministry with these words:

Take heed of destroying that which ye have begotten...That which calms and cools the spirit goes over the world and brings to the Father, to inherit the life eternal, and reaches to the spirits in prison in all. In the living unmovable word of the Lord God dwell, for whosoever goes out from the pure and ministers not in that, comes to an end; though he was serviceable for a time while he lived in the thing.

Take heed of many words; what reacheth to the life settles in the life...If Friends do not live in the life which they speak of, so that they answer the life in those they speak to, the other part steps in, and so there comes an acquaintance, and that comes over them.

As every one is kept in the life of God over all that is contrary, then he is in his place, he doth not lay hands on any suddenly. For if he doth he may lose his discerning, and lay hands on the wrong part and so let the deceit come near him and steal over; and it will be a hard thing for him to get it down. There is no one strikes his fellow-servant but first he is gone from the pure in his own particular. Then the Light which he is gone from, Christ, cometh and giveth him his reward. This is the state of evil servants. All the boisterous, hasty, and rash beget nothing to God; but the life, which doth reach the life, is that which begets to God...

Friends, be watchful and careful in all meetings ye come into. When a man is come newly out of the world he cometh out of the dirt. Then he must not be rash. For now when he cometh into a silent meeting, that is another state. Then he must come and feel his own spirit how it is, when he cometh to those that sit silent; for he may come in the heat of his spirit out of the world. Now the others are still and cool, and he may rather do them hurt if he get them out of the cool state into the heating state.[26]

This passage clearly shows that the prepared soul is capable of "going to weeds" and coming to no good end. Indeed, one of the most important features of the Quaker spirituality is the corporate life together.

Douglas Steere points to the primacy of the worshipping community when he notes:

...it is interesting that both the Eastern Orthodox and the Quakers look on the experience of the whole worshipping community gathered in corporate prayer as the truest organ for the operation of the Holy Spirit.[27]

Spiritual guidance consists in learning together how to know and live in this spirit. One central aspect is learning how to participate in the corporate gathering. Braithwaite suggests where the power of the corporate enterprise lay.

Throughout a chequered history of strength and weakness, it (Quakerism) has promoted retirement of heart and waiting upon the Lord as among the surest means for renewing spiritual strength.[28]

The genius of corporate nourishment for individual spirituality is this "waiting on the Lord," it is the key to spiritual guidance and effective Quaker service (*diakonia*) in the world, rather than a feared quietism lived out in despondency of spirit or passivity of individualistic piety.

Meditation was, perhaps, a luxury in more deliberate days: it is a necessity in ours. The lover of truth finds time for gazing upon it till the image is fixed in his soul. We are too often satisfied with being mere copyists or impressionists, — copyists because accomplishments and information are cheap substitutes for knowledge; impressionists, since prejudice is an easier guide than principle, and gushes of enthusiasm and sentiment than firmrooted purpose of heart. But the true wisdom needs deep ploughing and much silent and patient germination. It needs also that stillness of the flesh, which allows the sediment of worldly influences to settle, and gives time for the soul's apprehensions of truth to cohere and crystalize. Times of quiet worship and seasons for private retirement and prayer have a place of high value in the Christian life, though our Society of its devotion to these has at times neglected other human ministrations by which the hunger of the souls is aroused and satisfied.[29]

Braithwaite perceptively advises that one needs "deep ploughing and much silent and patient germination," which comes by waiting on the Lord. This is not like waiting for Godot where nothing happens.

Fox described this corporate nourishing of waiting as productive. The seed germinates, we are given the promise of God's love and relationship, and that promise is fulfilled.

Therefore, all wait patiently upon the Lord, whatsoever condition you be in; wait in the grace and truth that comes by Jesus; for if ye do so, there is a promise to you, and the Lord God will fulfill it in you. I have found it so, praised be the Lord who filleth with it, and satisfieth the desires of the hungry soul.[30]

In waiting on the Lord, the real truth emerges by the real Word being spoken. This makes obedience possible and ministry an actuality. Without waiting, one outruns the Guide or settles for conformity.

In this spirit of waiting upon the Lord, visitations of God's strength and power are given. Learning to live in this presence, means learning to "mind the light".[31] Indeed, this aspect of spiritual guidance may occupy the central portion of time among Friends. To mind the light is to walk in the light. It is to be on the journey with the same

Jesus who told his disciples, "I am the light of the world; he who follows me will not walk in darkness, but will have the light of life." (John 8:12)   To learn to walk in the light means more than theologically knowing about it. Spiritual guidance is that process of learning to live and love!

An example of the kind of work Fox did as spiritual director is found in his advice to Elizabeth Claypole in 1658. She was the daughter of Oliver Cromwell, but more importantly,   a very sick woman when Fox wrote to her. His advice was not only appropriate for her and her condition, but is sage advice for any person trying to live in the state of wholeness into which Christ calls us. Fox began by addressing her as Friend.

> Be still and cool in thy own mind and spirit from thy own thoughts, and then thou wilt feel the principle of God to turn thy mind to the Lord God, whereby thou wilt receive his strength and power from whence life comes, to allay all tempests, against blusterings and storms. That is it which moulds up into patience, into innocency, into soberness, into stillness, into staidness, into quietness, up to God, with his power. Therefore mind: that is the word of the Lord God unto thee... When (thou art in) the transgression of the life of God in the particular, the mind flies up in the air, and the creature is led into the night, and nature goes out of his course, and an old garment goes on, and an uppermost clothing, and nature leads out of his course, and so it comes to be all of a fire, in the transgression, and that defaceth the glory of the first body.
>
> Therefore be still a while from thy own thoughts, searching, seeking, desires and imaginations, and be stayed in the principle of God in thee, to stay thy mind upon God, up to God; and thou wilt find strength from him and (find him to) be present help in time of trouble, in need, and to be a God at hand. For all distractions, distempers, unruliness, confusion are in the transgression; which transgression must be brought down, before the principle of God, that hath been transgressed, be lifted up: whereby the mind may be seasoned and stilled in a right understanding of the Lord, whereby his blessing enters, and is felt over all that is contrary with the power of the Lord God, which gives dominion, which awakens the principle of God within,

which gives a feeling after God. Therefore, keep in the fear of the Lord God; that is the word of the Lord God unto thee. For all these things happen to thee for thy good and your good, to make you to know your own strength and means, and to know the Lord's strength and means, and to know the Lord's strength and power. Trust in him, therefore.[32]

This passage begins with that admonition to wait on the Lord in order to become centered in the principle of God. To come to the center is to be in the right place to mind the light. It is from this place, then, that Fox fully described the affective result of minding the light and living in the spirit.

In typical language of spiritual formation, Fox told Elizabeth the principle of God "moulds up" the character of a person. Spiritual direction is the graceful assistance one friend offers another as they get in touch with the Spirit who freshly fashions and molds them into servants of Christ. The light of Christ brings them to that place where the storms of the world would not overcome them. After all, their spirits have been free from their captivity of the earthly prison, and brought into the kingdom. Fox described this condition to Elizabeth with a series of terms: patience, innocency, soberness, stillness, staidness, quietness. These characteristics described not the bed of a sick woman, but the "condition" of a spiritually centered and healthy person. Spiritual guidance assists on the journey into this kind of health.

This distinction between spiritual health and joy in the midst of a suffering, painful world Fox and early Friends knew well and from this experience they offered spiritual guidance. In our own day, Thomas Merton has given voice to this kind of spirituality when he writes:

> ...you were created for spiritual JOY. And if you do not know the difference between pleasure and spiritual joy you have not yet begun to live.
>
> Life in this world is full of pain. But pain, which is the contrary of pleasure, is not necessarily the contrary of happiness or of joy. Because spiritual joy flowers in the full expansion of freedom that reaches out without obstacle to its supreme object, fulfilling itself in the perfect activity of disinterested love for which it was created.[33]

Spiritual guidance endeavors to inculcate joy and to witness the flowering of that joy in the full freedom of love. It is in this state Fox can admonish Elizabeth: "mind." "Mind God's word," that is, God's spiritual presence, because that is the source of joy and peace. "Feel after God," Fox told her. Then, Fox said not minding the light caused dis-ease, unrest and disharmony. In beautifully guiding phrases Fox began to detail the blind alleys of the spiritual journey when men and women become unattentive to the light.

He goes on to state that "the mind flies up in the air!" One sees here a picture of a person no longer rooted and grounded in God's principle. Instead of being anchored in the Spirit, she is now driven or cast adrift in the wind. Out of God's control means she will be tempted to resume "self-control" or "give up." This is captured in Fox's phrase, "the creature is led into the night." Not to be led by God does not mean one is not led! Rather, one is always led, and chooses between two options: God or Satan (or demons, phychoses, neuroses). Provocatively, Fox knew not being led by God means inevitably being led into the night of our demonic, destructive world, abandoning the security of Christ's hope grounded in faith for the illusion of something else.

In the night, more than any place, people of faith need what Alan Jones calls "the angels of God."[34] These are spiritual guides and friends who grace us with the truth that illusion is illusion, and compound this grace with the compassion of God's love incarnate. Once more in this ocean of darkness spiritually guiding people like Fox to Elizabeth will say, "deny thyself." "Then thou wilt feel the power of God...there thou wilt come to receive and feel the physician of value."[35] The physician is none other than the one who heals, who brings salvation and wholeness. Fox's final word to her, both the first word of faith and final word of love, is to *trust* God.

Trusting God seems easy in the flush of the early faith experience. The trying part of the journey of growth into spiritual maturity comes when the dry heat of summer withers the plants which germinate from the seed within. This, as well, is the most difficult place for spiritual guides. Quaker spirituality deals with this head on and labels these places "dry" periods or places. Part of discernment is knowing whether one, in fact, has fallen out of grace and re-entered the ocean of darkness, or whether one is yet in the ocean of light and life, but only in a dry place.

Dry periods are not just a Quaker problem but a spiritual problem. Fox encountered in Cleveland in 1651 a group of Ranters who had formerly "tasted of the power of God."[36] Fox described the manner in which they had "out-run the Spirit."

> Now they had had great meetings, so I told them after that they had had such meetings they did not wait upon God to feel his power to gather their minds together to feel his presence and power and therein to sit to wait upon him, for they had spoken themselves dry and had spent their portions and not lived in that which they spake, and now they were dry.[37]

This demonstrates clearly that the problem of being "dry" is different from having fallen back into the ocean of darkness. In this context, the spiritual guide does not admonish one to go back to the beginning, but rather to wait, to be still and let that divine principle again find one. Once more, Fox offered spiritual guidance to them in their dry place.

> ...my message unto them was from the Lord that they might all come together again and wait to feel the Lord's power and spirit in themselves to gather them to Christ and to be taught of him who says, 'Learn of me.' For after, when they had declared that which the Lord had opened to them, then the people were to receive it, and the speakers and they were to live in that themselves. But when they had not more to declare but to go to seek forms without life, that made themselves dry and barren and the people also. Thence came all their loss, for the Lord would renew his mercies and his strength if they would wait upon him.[38]

Over an extended period of time dry periods can render one lifeless and, eventually, relocate one in the ocean of darkness and death.

Fox describes these periods like a desert experience all over again. Feeling lost and alone in the wilderness, there is an accompanying sense of emptiness and dissatisfaction. There is also a frightening sense of impotence which comes from loosing the power and vitality which was once theirs in God's Spirit. In this state one knows that impotence betrays a barrenness, and that there is and will be no fruitfulness.

In another passage, Fox shifts the metaphor from dryness to frozenness. In an epistle to Friends in 1656 he warned them about potential dry periods.

> And Friends, though you may have tasted of the power and been convinced and have felt the light, yet afterwards you may feel winter storms, tempests, and hail, and be frozen, in frost and cold and a wilderness and temptations. Be patient and still in the power and still in the light that doth convince you, to keep your minds to God; in that be quiet, that you may come to the summer, that your flight be not in the winter. For if you sit still in the patience which overcomes in the power of God, there will be no flying. For the husbandman, after he hath sown his seed, he is patient. For by the power and by the light you will come to see through and feel over winter storms, tempests, and all the coldness, barrenness, emptyness. And the same light and power will go over the tempter's head, which power and light were before he was. And so in the light standing still you will see your salvation, you will see the Lord's strength, you will feel the small rain, you will feel the fresh springs in the power and light, your minds being kept low; for that which is out of the power and light lifts up. But in the power and light you will see God revealing his secrets, inspiring, and his gifts coming unto you, through which your hearts will be filled with God's love; praise to him that lives for ever more, in which light and power his blessings are received.'[39]

This passage reveals the master guide offering advice to confront these dry periods. First, there is the realism these winter storms are natural. It does not mean one has fallen back into the death of darkness. Be *patient*, counsels Fox and remain still in the light. This comes close to the advice given by a contemporary Friend as he describes the Quaker decision-making process. "'When in doubt, wait motto', painful as it may seem to the person or persons involved, has so often been found to test the flexibility and really centered spirit of the bearer of the concern."[40] In this waiting God will find us. Waiting upon the Lord does not mean passivity or lethargy of spirit. It means one cannot obey until one hears!

In waiting one will see spring follow the winter; one will see night give way to morning. To every drought, there comes rain. Stay where you are until you are told and know you are to move. In our contemporary time, Alan Jones best suggests what is at stake in this waiting.

> It takes considerable courage to wait in the dark between
> dreams and I don't know how it can be done without the
> grace of God and a struggling determination to trust him in
> the darkness. Nor can I envisage being able to wait for the
> coming of light without the supportive framework of friend-
> ship and community.[41]

Waiting will take God's grace to meet us and move us again. It takes
courage to wait and one of the roles of the spiritual guide is to encourage. The spiritual guide is "in it with us." He or she is a part of
the framework of friendship and community. Friends understand
every person needs this community and every one is this community
for the other. This is the essence of service, of ministry.

Quakers have lived out their service in the world in many ways.
Because there is that of God in every person, everyone is called to
a life of service. Spiritual direction is typically a key component in
the spiritual pilgrimage because it assists people to discover their
ministries and develop their gifts for these ministries. This book is
concerned with the nurturing experience which brings forth these
acts of service. The key is coming to know the light of Christ and,
then, minding that light. Contemporararily, Alan Jones puts words
to what was true for Fox, the earlier monastic tradition, and which
is rooted in the New Testament.

> The Christian heightens his or her awareness by sharing in
> what Paul calls "the mind of Christ." Prayer is an adventurous
> descent into that mind where, by the power of the Holy
> Spirit, our selfconsciousness is transfigured into Christ-
> consciousness. It is inevitably a way of sacrifice and self-
> surrender, a way not unlike the traditional call to monasti-
> cism. It is a creative way of poverty, chastity, and obedi-
> ence—poverty, because it means being truly poor before
> God; chastity, because it involves a single—minded devo-
> tion to him; obedience, because our single-minded attention
> will be manifested in specific acts of love. This threefold way
> is one of submission, of sacrifice and surrender for the sake
> of the more abundant life. The three traditional monastic
> vows provide us with some clues about the way in which all
> Christians are called to respond to the freedom offered them

in Christ. They are the marks of Christ himself and subsequently the marks of those who follow him. Poverty, chastity, and obedience are also the marks of a good spiritual guide and friend of the soul.[42]

Ministry issues out of this "Christ-consciousness." Through a life of prayer one comes into communication with God. In this prayer-ful relationship the spoken word of God is inevitably heard. Having heard, one *obeys*.

The obvious goal of spiritual guidance is growing closer to God who loves us. This deepening relationship calls for sacrificing one's old self's habits and desiring surrender to the lover's will. Spiritual guidance plays a crucial role in this call to ministry. There is always an urgency—even in the waiting. Overlooking the sexist language one can see the brilliance of Braithwaite's insight when he declared that:

> The matter of urgency now was to re-awaken spiritual re-sponsiveness on the part of the individual, to give the young men vision and service, to fix the thought of the church not on itself but on its mission, so that both in the body as a whole and in its several members the call of the Lord might be known and obeyed.[43]

The call and obedience go together. To obey means to "hear." Hearing is not simply an auditory phenomenon. Indeed, it might be just a still, small voice. The key to obedience and ministry is that one is *moved*. In Quaker spirituality there is a great deal of emphasis on *movement*. This is the fitting sequel to waiting on the Lord. Waiting leads to movement which is obedience.

A good example of this action of God in lives comes from a period in 1670 when Fox was very ill. In fact, rumor had it that Fox was dead! But, Fox replied, "the next news they heard I was gone twelve miles in a coach to Gerard Roberts who was very weak, which astonished them to hear it. And I was moved to speak to him and encourage him, though I could hardly hear or see."[44] In that same period Fox also travelled to Enfield to see Amor Stoddard who also was quite sick.

> I was moved to tell him he had been faithful as a man and faithful to God and that the immortal Seed of life was his crown, and with many others words I was moved to speak

to him though I was so weak I was hardly able to stand.[45]

What Fox said about being moved to speak is standard for how Quakers portray the inner workings of God's spirit in their lives.

Like the wind, the spirit moves freshly within and one can feel it, know it and obey it. With this image comes a sense of energy and dynamism. In fact, spiritual stagnation or stasis is not possible. The call of God is a call to be pilgrim, to be on a journey, to move. The Spirit and the Spirit's guides offer a sense of direction, but one must move. Ministry is the result of this movement. Movement is obedience—obedience to speak revelationally, to live revolutionally, to act powerfully.

The Quaker testimonies on behalf of peace, simplicity, etc. are rooted in this movement of the Spirit. Fox said:

> That the spirit of Christ, by which we are guided, is not changeable, so as once to command us from a thing as evil and again to move into it...that the spirit of Christ, which leads us into all Truth, will never move us to fight and war against any man with outward weapons, neither for the kingdom of Christ, nor for the kingdom of the world.[46]

Or, in Fox's word which became the basis of a contemporary song, "we cannot learn war any more."[47]

Not to learn war any more is radical. Christians moved by the Spirit will be called into radical ministry. In the face of God, and maybe even in the eyes of the world, one is stripped of egoistic pretense and given the Shekinah of gracious protection. We are able in this protective garb to be fools for Christ. To this foolish end, Fox said:

> And many have been moved to go naked in their streets as signs of their nakedness. And many men and women have been moved to go naked and in sackcloth, in the other power's days and since, as signs of their nakedness from the image of God and righteousness and holiness, and how that God would strip them and make them bare and naked as they were.[48]

To be stripped naked strikes those in the modern world as either crazy or stupid. We are too controlled, too sophisticated, to give into any *movement* which displaces individual control or upsets corporate culture.

Braithwaite wrote almost a century ago, "we prefer the security of stagnation to the dangers and glory of vigorous life."[49] To be moved by this spirit into witness and ministry is to be moved to become imitators of Christ. Anytime this occurs, one knows the place of the cross of Christ. Fox could not have been more clear about anything than that the cross stood at the meeting place of the Spirit and the world. To obey God's word is to hear the call to sacrifice. The call to sacrifice embraces a ministry which asks for the death of self in the transcending care for the other. The sacrificial ministry of love risks death and receives the delight of resurrection. In this sense, ministry is always creative; the Seed always produces more seeds. In Alan Jones' words:

> The very act of creation is sacrificial. The reaching out which every creative act requires is a breaking open of the self. Without the breaking open of the self there is no delight! How can there be if the self is trapped inside itself? Sacrifice is exposure. It is vulnerability. This is what drives us. This is the energy that makes us tick.[50]

The Spirit always moves one to the center; the center is Christ and the cross. Living in the Spirit means sacrificial commitment. Walking in the Spirit means moving out of the ocean of death to walk on the waters of life.

Sacrifice is *exposure*. Ministry always declares, in Fox's words, "this power is the Cross, in which mystery of the Cross is the fellowship; and this the Cross in which is the true and everlasting glorying, which crucifies from all other glorying."[51] Sacrifice is *vulnerability*. vulnerability means the potential to get hurt. The sacrifice of the cross certainly means hurt. Consequently, too often a spirituality is constructed which tips the hat to the illusion of vulnerability while maintaining sufficient distance from the passionate God to remain safe. We would settle for being liked rather than loved!

Urban Holmes' indictment of ordained clergy applies to all Christians called to ministry. He says:

> ...it has become almost a cliche that the ordained person is not called to be successful, but to be faithful. Fidelity requires above all an openness that leaves us terribly vulnerable. Every effort to protect that vulnerability requires

us to deny our vocation.[52]

A threat to ministry is to protect ourselves from vulnerability, to become protected risks denying our vocation. Quaker spirituality refuses to allow the church to limit the vocation of ministry to a "state of ordination." Ministry is the vocation of all. Vulnerability is its fear. Nakedness is its sign. Community is its support. Finally, love is its reward.

This love will be to us a blessing and the blessing an anointment into the kingdom. In the freedom of this vocation of loving service we will "walk cheerfully over the world, answering that of God in every one...Then to the Lord God you will be a sweet savour and a blessing."[53]

Notes

Preface

1. John Punshon, *Encounter With Silence*, (Richmond, IN.: Friends United Press, 1987), p. 17.

2. James Breech, *The Silence of Jesus*, (Augsburg Fortess, Minneapolis, MN.: 1946) p. 3.

3. Graham Greene, *The Power and The Glory*, (New York, NY. Viking Penguin, 1990) p. 130.

4. Ibid.

Introduction

1. Douglas V. Steere, *Quaker Spirituality*, (New York: Paulist Press, 1984), pp. 4-5.

2. Adolf Harnack, *What Is Christianity?*, trans. by Thomas Bailey Saunders, (New York: Harper and row, 1957.)

3. Urban T. Holmes, *Spirituality for Ministry*, (San Francisco: Harper and Row, 1982), p. 9.

4. Alice Walker, "God is Inside You and Inside Everbody Else", in *Weaving the Visions*, ed. Judity Plaskow and Carol P. Christ, (San Francisco: Harper and Row, 1989), p. 103.

5. Henry David Thoreau, *Walden* in *The Portable Thoreau*, ed. by Carl Bode. (New York: Penguin Books, 1977), p. 263.

6. Urban T. Homes, III, *A History of Christian Spirituality*, (New York: The Seabury Press, 1981), p. 1.

7. Malcolm Muggeridge, *Christ and the Media*, (Grand Rapids, MI: Wm. B. Eerdmans, 1977), pp. 54-5.

8. Ibid., p. 30.

9. Parker T. Palmer, *To Know As We Are Known*, (San Francisco: Harper and Row, 1983), p. 14.

10. John L. Nickalls, ed., *The Journal of George Fox*, (Cambridge: Harper and Row, 1983), p. 14.

11. Joann Wolski Conn, *Spirituality and Personal Maturity*, (Mahwah, N.J.: Paulist Press, 1989), p. 13.

12. Abraham Joshua Heschel, *Quest for God*, (New York: Crossroad, Paulist Press, 1989), p. xi.

13. Ibid., p. xii. (preserving the non-inclusive language when quoting)

14. Wendy M. Wright, "Reflections on Spiritual Friendship between Men and Women," *Weavings*, Vol. 2. No. 4, 1987, p. 21.

15. Murray Bodo, "Advice for Spiritual Joggers," *Catholic Update*, (Cincinnati: St. Anthony Messenger Press, 1979), p. 2.

16. Ibid., p. 4.

17. Heschel, p. 11.

18. Thomas R. Kelly, *A Testament of Devotion*, (New York: Harper and Row, 1941), p. 51.

19. Walter Wink, *Naming the Powers*, (Philadelphia: Fortress Press, 1984), p. 111.

20. Palmer, p. 12.

Chapter 1. The Ocean of Darkness

1. Fox, *Journal of George Fox*, (Friends United Press. 1908 ed.) p. 19.

2. Sallie MacFague, *Metaphorical Theology: Models of God in Religious Language*, (Philadelphia: Fortress Press, 1982), p. 42.

3. Gerald May, *Care of Mind/Care of Spirit: Psychiatric Dimentions of Spiritual Direction*, (San Francisco: Harper and Row, 1982), p. 42.

4. Alan Jones, *Exploring Spiritual Direction: An Essay on Christian Friendship*, (New York: The Seabury Press, 1982), p. 56.

5. Fox, p.1.

6. Ibid.

7. Thomas Merton, *New Seeds of Contemplation*, (New York: New Directions Publishing Corporation, 1972) p. 25.

8. Fox, p. 3.

9. Ibid, p. 10; see also p. 3.

10. Fox, p. 4.

11. Benedict J. Groeschel, *Spiritual Passages: The Psychology of Spiritual Development*, (New York: Crossroad, 1986), p. 131.

12. May, p. 90. See pp. 90-91 for a more detailed comparison of the experience of the spiritual dark night and the psychological experience of depression and despair.

13. Fox, pp. 5-6

14. Ibid., pp. 9-10.
15. Richard J. Foster, *Celebration of Discipline: The Path to Spiritual Growth*, (New York: Harper and Row, 1978), p. 41.
16. Ibid, p. 48.
17. Alan Jones, *Soul Making: The Desert Way of Spirituality*, (New York: Harper and Row, 1985), p. 89.
18. Sebastian Moore, *The Inner Loneliness* (New York: Crossroad, 1982), p. 67.
19. Henri J.M. Nouwen, *The Way of the Heart: Desert Spirituality and Contemporary Ministry*, (New York: Seabury Press, 1981), pp. 27-28.
20. Ibid, p. 25.
21. Fox, p. 12.
22. Wink, p. 142.
23. Fox, p. 6.
24. Merton, p. 275.
25. May, pp. 72-73.
26. Fox, p. 33.
27. Ibid., pp. 14-15.
28. Malachi 3:1-2: Behold I send my messenger to prepare the way before me, and the Lord whom you seek will suddenly come to his temple; the messenger of the covenant in whom you delight, behold, he is coming, says the Lord of hosts. But who can endure the day of his coming, and who can stand when he appears? For he is like a refiner's fire and like fullers' soap.
29. Quakers have rightly been seen to have an influence from John's gospel. But what unfortunately has been overlooked is the heavy reliance of Fox and early Friends on the apostle Paul. No where is this more significant than in Fox's use of Paul's flesh/spirit typology. A good example of the Pauline typology is a passage from Galatians. "But I say, walk by the Spirit, and do not gratify the desires of the flesh. For the desires of the flesh are against the Spirit, and the desires of the Spirit are against the flesh..."(5:16-17) In many ways it is not helpful to point out this Pauline influence because Paul himself is so often misunderstood by Christians. And yet on this flesh/spirit motif some understanding is helpful. Although both terms can refer to "parts" of the human being, the way Paul also uses these terms is how Fox uses them, as synonyms for the two oceans. "Flesh" and "spirit" are two modes of existence, two ways of living...without God and with God. Herman Ridderbos, *Paul: An Outline of His Theology*, trans. John Richard DeWitt (Grand Rapids, MI: Wm. B. Eerdmans, 1975), p. 66. says "'flesh' and 'Spirit' represent two modes of existence, on the one hand that of the old aeon which is characterized and determined by the flesh, on the other that of the new creation which is of the Spirit of God...the contrast is therefore of a redemptive-historical nature..." This is extemely important because it shows the central role Jesus Christ plays as transformer of the old aeon. For Fox, Jesus Christ was the

one to bring him out of the ocean of darkness and death into the ocean of light and love.

30. See footnote 7.

31. Merton, p. 24.

32. Jones, *Soul Making*, p. 64.

33. Thomas Merton, *Contemplative Prayer*, (Garden City, N.Y.: Image Books, 1971), p. 24.

34. Elfrida Vipont, *A Faith To Live By*, (Philadelphia: Friends General Conference, 1962), p. 11.

Chapter 2. Brokenness of Heart

1. Fox, pp. 20-21.

2. Jones, *Soul Making*, p. 65.

3. Merton, *Contemplative Prayer*, p. 24.

4. Fox, pp. 569-570.

5. Ibid., p. 11.

6. Paul Tillich, *Systematic Theology*, 3 vols. (Chicago: University of Chicago Press, 1967), II:44-45.

7. Ibid., II-49.

8. Jones, *Soul Making*, p. 199.

9. Merton, *Contemplative Prayer*, pp. 24-25.

10. Fox, p. 283.

11. Groeschel, p. 73.

12. See Walter Conn, *Christian Conversion: A Developmental Interpretation of Autonomy and Surrender* (Mahwah, NJ: Paulist press, 1986), p. 188, who cites V. Bailey Gillespie, *Religious Conversion and Personal Identity: How and Why People Change* (Birmingham AL: Religious Education Press, 1979), pp. 47-57. There Conn suggests three phases in "the personal experience of religious conversion." They are "(1)preconversion, with questioning tension, anxiety, and stress; (2)crisis, with the sense of a greater presence, higher control, and self-surrender; (3)postconversion, with its relief, release, assurance, harmony, peace, ecstatic happiness. Whatever the language used, the conflict resolution of conversion, from a functional perspective, is both problem-solving and identity-forming."

13. Ibid., p. 133.

14. May, *Care of Mind*, p. 20.

15. Tillich, I:191.

16. Ibid.

17. Ibid., I:191, footnote 7.

18. Fox, p. 1.

19. Merton, *New Seeds*, p. 180.

20. Fox, p. 4.

21. Ibid.

22. Ibid., pp 4-5.

23. Eugene H. Peterson, *Working the Angles: The Shape of Pastoral Integrity*, (Grand Rapids, MI: William B. Eerdmans, 1987), p. 122.

24. Martin Thornton, *Spiritual Direction: A Practical Introduction* (London: SPCIC, 1984), p. 96. He defines *attrait* as "a person's natural spiritual propensity, his inclination towards or attraction to particular forms of prayer; hence the sort of prayer, spiritual outlook, or theological direction that comes most naturally to him," p. 32.

25. Fox, p. 15.

26. Ibid., p. 16.

27. Ibid.

28. Nouwen, *The Way of the Heart*, p. 28.

29. Ibid.

30. See footnote 12.

31. Merton, *New Seeds*, p. 160.

32. John Climacus, *The Ladder of Divine Ascent*, trans. by Colm Luibheid and Jorman Russell (New York: Paulsit Press, 1982), p. 74.

33. Ibid.

34. Ibid., p. 75.

35. Ibid., p. 76.

36. Fox, p. 21.

37. Jones, *Soul Making*, pp. 48-49.

38. Rosemary Haughton, *The Passionate God*, (Ramsey, NJ: Paulist Press, 1981), p. 124.

39. Ibid.

40. Merton, *New Seeds*, pp. 108-109.

41. Bette Midler, *The Rose*.

42. Haughton, p. 125.

43. Climacus, pp. 81-82.

44. Climacus, p. 86.

45. Ibid.

46. Ibid., p. 85.

47. Ibid.

48. Merton, *Contemplative Prayer*, p. 27.

49. Nouwen, *The Way of the Heart*, p. 22.

50. Haughton, pp. 4-5.

51. Ibid., p. 60.

52. Ibid.

Chapter 3. My Heart Did Leap For Joy

1. Fox, p. 11.

2. Jones, *Soul Making*, pp. 23-4.

3. Thornton, *Spiritual Direction*, p. 32.

4. Ibid., characterizes the speculative mode of spirituality as more intellectual, more formal, more inclined to disciplined duty. For purposes here, it might be instructive to hear Thornton say the line of speculatives include "A great body of Anglican divines: true piety and sound learning, or in less conventional language, don't let your heart run away with your head." (p. 33)

5. McFague, *Metaphorical Theology*, p. 39.

6. Ibid.

7. WalterConn, p. 188. Conn is still using Gillespie's analysis. See chapter 2, footnote 12.

8. Ibid.

9. Ibid.

10. Ibid.

11. Ibid., p. 193.

12. Ibid., p. 209.

13. Fox, p. 7.

14. Ibid.

15. Langdon Gilkey, *Message and Existence: An Introduction to Christian Theology*, (New York: The Seabury Press, 1979), pp. 43-44.

16. Ibid., p. 44.

17. Fox, p. 8.

18. Haughton, p. 218.

19. Fox, p. 9.

20. Georges Florovsky, *Bible, Church, Tradition: An Eastern Orthodox View*, vol. I, in Collected Works of Georges Florovsky (Belmont, MA: Nordland Pulishing Co., 1972), p. 36.

21. Steere, p. 6.

22. See quotation 19.

23. Fox, pp. 11-12.

24. Ibid., p. 14.

25. Holmes, *A History of Christian Spirituality*, p. 135.

26. See page 19. Fox, p. 20.

27. Fox, p. 21.

28. Jones, *Soul Making*, p. 48 (See p. 50 for full quotation).

29. Haughton, p. 153.

30. Fox, pp. 11-12. (Quoted earlier in this chapter on p. 53.)

31. Ibid., p. 14. (Quoted earlier in this chapter on p. 54).

32. Jones, *Soul Making*, p. 110.

33. Fox, pp. 13-14.

Chapter 4. The Ocean of Light

1. Fox, p. 19.

2. Ibid., p. 117.

3. Ibid., p. 210.

4. M. Robert Mulholland, Jr., *Shaped by the Word: The Power of Scripture in Spiritual Formation*, (Nashville: The Upper Room, 1985) pp. 110-112.

5. Fox, p. 22.

6. Ibid., p. 117. See fuller quotation on p. 62 of this chapter.

7. Ibid., pp. 27-28.

8. Ibid., p. 18.

9. Ibid.

10. Ibid., p. 367.

11. Ibid., pp. 267-8.

12. Ibid. p. 368. See also, p. 216, for perfection as being made clean.

13. Ibid., p. 120.

14. Ibid., p. 344, see footnote 2.

15. Ibid., p. 335.

16. Ibid., p. 336.

17. Ibid., p. 116.

18. Ibid., p. 115.

19. Ibid., p. 283. See also p. 24 for a continued citation of this passage.

20. Ibid., p. 74.

21. Ibid., p. 78.

22. Ibid., p. 328.

23. Ibid., p. 329.

24. Ibid.

25. Ibid., p. 283.

26. See p. 62 (quoting *Journal*, p. 117.)

27. Ibid., p. 309.

28. Tillich, III:403.

29. Ibid.

30. Fox, p. 193.

31. Ibid., p. 279.

32. Lewis Benson, *What Did George Fox Teach About Christ? New Foundation Publications*, no. 1 (Gloucester, Eng: George Fox Fund, 1976), p. 3.

33. Fox, p. 271.

34. Ibid.

35. Ibid.

36. Thomas R. Kelly, *A Testament of Devotion*, (New York: Harper and Row, 1941) p. 30.

37. See note 31.

38. Fox, p. 294.

41. Gerald G. May, *Addiction and Grace*,   (San Francisco: Harper and Row, 1988), p. 120.

42. Hugh Barbour, *The Quakers in Puritan England*, (New Haven: Yale University, Press, 1964), p. 98.

43. Ibid., p. 103.

44. Kelly, p. 53.

45. Ibid., p. 33-34.

Chapter 5. A Great People To Be Gathered

1. Fox, pp. 103-104.

2. Elfrida Vipont, *George Fox and the Valiant Sixty*, (London, Hamish Hamilton, 1975) p. 18.

3. Ibid.

4. Fox, p. 105.

5. Norman Perrin, *The Resurrection According to Matthew, Mark and Luke*, (Philadelphia: Fortress Press, 1977), p. 3.

6. See Acts 2:37-42 for the response to the original Pentecost. For the other traditional (but less well-known) account of Pentecost read John 20:19-23.

7. Fox, p. 104.

8. Ibid., p. 302.

9. Ibid., p. 354.

10. Ibid., p. 15.

11. Ibid., p. 16.

12. Ibid., p. 107.

13. Steere, p. 37.

14. Fox, p. 24.

15. Ibid., p. 94.

16. Ibid., p. 283.

17. Ibid., p. 126.

18. Haughton, p. 329.

19. Margaret R. Miles, *Fullness of Life: Historical Foundations for a New Asceticism*, (Philadelphia: Westminster Press, 1981), p. 143.

20. Ibid.

21. Fox, p. 574.

22. Ibid., p. 578.

23. Ibid.

24. Walter Brueggermann, *Praying the Psalms*, (Winona, MN: Saint Mary's Press, 1982) p. 47.

25. Fox, p. 301.

26. Ibid., p. 545.

27. This Pauline influence underscores the apocalyptic context of seventeenth century England which formed Fox's sense of mission. Pauline

27. This Pauline influence underscores the apocalyptic context of seventeenth century England which formed Fox's sense of mission. Pauline influence especially informed Fox's understanding of mission leading to transformation. In an apocalyptic context, transformation made one a son or daughter of God and, hence, placed one in a new age. In Romans 8:22-23 Paul said, "We know that the whole creation has been groaning in travail together until now; and not only the creation, but we ourselves, who have the first fruits of the Spirit, groan inwardly as we wait for adoption as sons, the redemption of our bodies." For Fox, this "now" of adoption has happened and in this, seems to move beyond Paul and a strict apocalyptic context. But even for Fox, there is the "not yet" of the kingdom. There is more work to be done as God's missionary agents of liberation—for other people and the whole creation. Doug Gwyn captures very well the essence of the relationship of transformation and mission in an apocalyptic context when he says "The insistent, New Testament emphasises that one must die to the self and be born anew to God, is made within this cosmic horizon; the individual participates in the cosmic transformation that God has promised...a new heaven and a new earth." Douglas Gwyn, *Apocalypse of the Word*, Richmond, IN., Friends United Press, 1984), p. 160.

28. Fox, p. 34.

29. Ibid., p. 44.

30. Ibid., pp. 34-35.

31. Benson, p. 2. (See p. 78.)

32. Ibid., p. 3.

33. Barbour, p. 110.

34. Fox, p. 274.

35. Thomas Merton, *The Monastic Journey*, ed. Brother Patrick Hart (Garden City, NY: Image Books, 1978), p. 83.

36. Ibid.

37. Kelly, pp. 96-97.

38. Tillich, III:111-112.

39. Fox, p. 38.

40. See the statement in Steere's, *Quaker Spirituality*, p. 18, to the effect that "the pansacramental sense of the holiness of every life relationship is also intimately connected with this inward experience of communion.

41. Tillich, III:112.

42. Fox, p. 302.

43. Benson, p. 17.

44. Fox, p. 27.

45. Merton, *Monastic Journey*, p. 43.

46. Fox, p. 174.

47. Haughton, p. 324.

Chapter 6. Walk Cheerfully Over the World

1. Fox, p. 263.

2. *Peace Pilgrim, Her Life and Work in Her Own Words*, (Santa Fe, NM: 1983), p. 56.

3. Ibid., p. 87.

4. Fox, p. 11.

5. John Punshon, *Portrait in Grey: A Short History of the Quakers*, (London: Quaker Home Service, 1984), p 63.

6. Alaistair Campbell, *Rediscovering Pastoral Care*, (Philadelphia: The Westminster Press, 1981), p. 27.

7. See the initial chapter of May, *Care of the Mind, Care of Spirit*.

8. Thomas Merton, *Spiritual Direction and Meditation* (Collegeville, MN: The Liturgical Press, 1960), p. 13.

9. May, *Care of Mind, Care of Spirit*, p. 1.

10. Ibid., p. 7.

11. William C. Braithwaite, *Spiritual Guidance in Quaker Experience*, (London: Woodbrooke Extension Committee, 1909), p. 33.

12. Jones, *Exploring Spiritual Direction*, p. 1-2.

13. Ibid., p. 4.

14. Bodo, p. 2.

15. Braithwaite, p. 82.

16. Ibid., p. 44.

17. Fox, p. 263. See p. 109 for full citation of this quotation.

18. Ibid., p. 183.

19. Ibid., p. 152.

20. Gwyn, p. 53.

21. Fox, p. 152. See p. 116 again for full citation of this text.

22. Gwyn, p. 131.

23. Braithwaite, p. 73.

24. Fox, p. 339.

25. Ibid., p. 338.

26. Ibid., p. 340.

27. Steere, p. 28.

28. Braithwaite, p. 81.

29. Ibid., pp. 90-91.

30. Fox, pp. 12-13.

31. See, for example, Fox, p. 135.

32. Ibid., pp. 346-347.

33. Merton, *New Seeds*, p. 259.

34. Jones, *Soul Making*, p. 51.

35. Fox, p. 347.

36. Ibid., p. 79.

37. Ibid.

40. Steere, p. 46.

41. Jones, *Exploring Spiritual Direction*, p. 68.

42. Ibid. For a full treatment of these themes by a contemporary Quaker see Richard J. Foster, *Money, Sex and Power: The Challenge of the Disciplined Life*, (San Francisco: Harper and Row).

43. Braithwaite, p. 77-78.

44. Fox, p. 571.

45. Ibid.

46. Ibid., pp. 399-400.

47. Ibid., p. 402.

48. Ibid., p. 503.

49. Braithwaite, p. 74.

50. Jones, *Exploring Spiritual Direction*, p. 117.

51. Fox, p. 283.

52. Holmes, *Spirituality for Ministry*, p. 117.

53. Fox, p. 263.